A MARRIAGE GUIDE FOR THE YOUNG ADULT

I WANT TO MARRY YU BUT...

Jennifer Yeo

A MARRIAGE GUIDE FOR THE YOUNG ADULT

I WANT TO MARRY YU

BUT...

WS Education

Published by

World Scientific Publishing Co. Pte. Ltd.

5 Toh Tuck Link, Singapore 596224

USA office: 27 Warren Street, Suite 401-402, Hackensack, NJ 07601

UK office: 57 Shelton Street, Covent Garden, London WC2H 9HE

Library of Congress Cataloging-in-Publication Data
Yeo, Jennifer.
   I want to marry you but -- : a marriage guide for the young adult / Jennifer Yeo.
     p. cm.
  ISBN-13: 978-9814407939
  ISBN-10: 9814407933
  1. Domestic relations--Handbooks, manuals, etc. 2. Matrimonial actions--
Handbooks, manuals, etc.
I. World Scientific Publishing Co. II. Title.
  K670.Y46 2014
  346.01'6--dc23

                                        2012015865

British Library Cataloguing-in-Publication Data
A catalogue record for this book is available from the British Library.

Cover concept by Zhang Xiuying

Desk Editor: Lum Pui Yee

Typeset by Stallion Press
Email: enquiries@stallionpress.com

Printed in Singapore by B & Jo Enterprise Pte Ltd

Disclaimer

This book is for informative purposes only. While due care has been taken to ensure the accuracy of the contents, this book does not purport to provide a complete or authoritative statement of law and does not constitute legal advice and/or any representation made by the author, Jennifer Yeo, her team and/or the publisher. No person should rely on the contents of this publication without first obtaining advice from a qualified professional.

Although Jennifer Yeo, her editorial team and the publisher have made every effort to ensure that the information in this book was correct at the press time, the author, her editorial team and publisher do not assume and hereby disclaim any liability to any party for any loss, damage or disruption caused by errors or omissions, whether such errors or omissions result from negligence or any other cause.

Illustrative quotes used in this book are merely those that the author objectively believes represent the chapter or section. The author, her editorial team and the publisher do not warrant that the quotes cited are accurate depictions of the chapter or section.

All non-Muslim marriages in Singapore are governed by the Women's Charter (Cap. 353).[1] Muslim marriages are governed by the Administration of Muslim Law Act (Cap. 3) which is a separate legislation from the Women's Charter. Hence, Muslim marriages have not been discussed in this book.

---

[1] s 3(4) Women's Charter (Cap. 353)

The author and the publisher have made every effort to trace and acknowledge sources/resources/individuals with respect to the quotes above. In the event that any information has been incorrectly attributed or credited, the author welcomes correspondence from those individuals/companies whom we have been unable to trace and acknowledge. Any omissions brought to our attention will be rectified at the earliest opportunity.

To all the wonderful men and women
who made this book possible

Contents

Acknowledgements

This book is the culmination of almost three years of research, brainstorming, developing concepts and ideas, writing and re-writing chapters on the subject of marriage. Words cannot express my heartfelt gratitude to the people who spent countless hours producing the draft manuscripts, and sitting in with me at meetings whilst juggling their ongoing work, and discussing our thoughts, aspirations and direction for the book.

My sincere thanks go out to Madan Mohan, who was instrumental in creating a first draft. I am also thankful to the two Relevant Legal Trainees who worked hard at the second draft and requested to remain anonymous. Thanks also to Chan Yi Hui Isabel Eva, and Lim Hui Ting Loretta. My appreciation also goes out to Dr Miles Rzechowicz, Gerthrine Cheo, Will Yong and Mrs Janice Woon for their helpful suggestions and comments in the early stage.

I am thankful for the constructive input of the following people. They helped in the rewriting, editing, research and corrections:

Chapters One and Two: Rosita Ng Pek Yeng, Ronald Midian Susilo, Rachel Tan Ying Ying, Ho Pearl

Chapters Three: Lawrence Khoo Kah Han, Javern Sim Jun Yan, Adeline Sim

Chapters Four and Five: Ho Pearl, Liew Hui Yan, Tham Kai Mun

Chapters Six: Valerie Loh Eng Jong, Javern Sim Jun Yan

A special mention should be made of Rosita Ng Pek Yeng for helping me to coordinate much of the earlier work and Ronald Midian Susilo for contributing the first draft on prenuptial agreements. Very special thanks to Ho Pearl for her constant and tireless efforts in helping me to manage, coordinate and edit the research, contents and footnotes as well as proof reading and compliance with intellectual property laws.

I am grateful for the administrative support for the book provided by Kong Sue-Anne, Alice Gan, Brinden Anandakumar, Jessie Chu, Felicia Lua and Su Vien Tan, who were instrumental in liaising with the World Scientific Team, arranging for meetings, and coordinating group efforts. I also thank Brinden Anandakumar and Adeline Sim for doing further research and for helping with the footnote renumbering and Jasselyn Seet, Sean Lee and Hsiang Cheng Wen for updating the research, content and footnotes and proofreading the book.

My humble thanks and appreciation also go out to the World Scientific Team, Dr KK Phua, Mrs Doreen Phua, Christopher Yow, Lum Pui Yee, Max Phua and Nee Phua who patiently supported and nurtured the production and publication of this project till its fruition today. Thank you for encouraging us till the finish line. Also, a big thank you to Zhang Xiuying who designed the delightful book cover for this project.

I am grateful that you, dear reader, are reading this work. I hope that you will glean some practical advice that will prove to be useful to you and that it will be a source of blessing in your life.

Last but not least, thanks be to God from whom all blessings come.

Foreword

Marriage is like signing a 356-page contract without knowing what is in it.

— *Kenneth Blanchard*

Marriage changes your life forever. It is a lifetime commitment based on a bond of love and one should enter this institution willing to give oneself up to a lifetime of loving service to one's spouse and children. Marriage is a wonderful institution that provides a safe harbour within which the couple can develop to their full potential in every area of their lives and together build a family within which they can find solace and companionship in the journey of life. Marriage enables the couple to experience humanity with all its agonies and ecstasies to live out their different roles as friends, lovers, parents, and providers. A couple in a marriage can help each other become better persons, overcome their fears, correct their flaws and strive for happiness. This union is complete in the physical, spiritual and emotional dimensions and the role of the law is to provide the parameters and guidance on how people should behave in a marriage as a couple and as parents.

Kenneth Blanchard once said that marriage is like signing a 356-page contract without knowing what is in it. Alarmingly, many young couples impulsively enter into it without considering or knowing what is involved or the legal, economic and social consequences. Many have come to grief, resulting in rising divorce numbers and people who choose cohabitation over marriage.

This book aims to explain simply the significance of marriage between spouses. It aspires to explain and simplify the many intricate legal issues attached to family law in Singapore. The book is not meant to be an exhaustive elucidation of family law or a scholarly and academic treatise. As a friendly guide for the layman, it is hoped that couples will find it a useful compendium to refer to from time to time and it is hoped, dear reader, that you will, like me, want to present a copy to each of your children to encourage them to have longlasting and successful marriages.

The chapters on divorce, custody of children and division of assets are included to alert couples to the red flags and potential pitfalls in a marriage.

It is hoped that this book can be a humble guide and companion to the couple in search of marital bliss and happiness.

Jennifer Yeo

Chapter One

The First Step: Single and Dating

A relationship isn't going to make me survive. It's the cherry on top.
— Jennifer Aniston

During the dating process, the couple should try to spend more time together so that they can find out as much as possible about each other to see if they are compatible and share similar values.

During my youth, the usual progression of the relationship is as follows: casual dating which is not exclusive followed by "going steady" which is in effect exclusive dating, then the engagement (with a view to marriage) culminating in the marriage and exchange of vows "till death do us part" which ought to be final and irrevocable and made with the greatest solemnity and utmost commitment.

The whole object of the courting process is to see if love grows between the two. I believe that the couple needs a big store of love to see the marriage through to the end of their lives.

Couples who are dating may be tempted to cohabit before or instead of getting married. The idea of an unmarried couple "setting up home together" appears to have lost some of the stigma previously associated with it. Cohabitation is even viewed by some as part of the process of getting to know and understand the other better and as a prelude to marriage.[1]

However, should the couple break up after cohabiting, there is a risk that the couple could be stigmatised by their "history". Future relationships could also be adversely affected. Further, what they thought of as a "no-strings-attached" relationship would in reality have spiritual, emotional, psychological, social and economic consequences. The couple should abstain from sexual intimacy because they should concentrate on building the emotional intimacy before marriage.

COHABITATION WITHOUT MARRIAGE

There is no legal definition of the concept of cohabitation. Instead, there is the common perception that cohabitation refers to an arrangement where two unmarried people in an emotionally and/or sexually intimate relationship live together similar to a spousal relationship.

A couple who plans to cohabit must be aware that they will not be accorded similar privileges as legally married counterparts. In the eyes of the law, a cohabiting couple is treated like strangers living in the same household.

There are a few points all couples planning to cohabit ought to take note of:

- **Financial Support:** There is no legal obligation for cohabitants to support each other financially. Should the couple separate, the court will not have the same power to order monthly maintenance and distribution of assets as a family court would, as matrimonial laws would not apply to the cohabitants.

---

[1] In a recent survey commissioned by the Institute of Policy Studies, "66% of the respondents felt it acceptable for a man and woman to live together before registering for marriage." The reason given by the majority of those who were willing to cohabit before marriage was the opportunity to get to know and understand the other better. See "IPS Perception of Policies in Singapore (POPS) Survey 6: Perceptions of singles on Marriage and Having Children, Jun 2013" at http://lkyspp.nus.edu.sg/ips/wp-content/uploads/sites/2/2013/06/POPS-6_Aug-12_report.pdf. The survey was commissioned to "understand the attitudes and perceptions of single Singaporean residents towards marriage, family and parenthood, including their perspectives on pre-martial cohabitation and having children out of wedlock."

In comparison, a husband is legally bound to maintain for his wife during the marriage. If the marriage breaks down, the court has the right to divide the matrimonial assets and impose a continuing obligation on the husband to maintain his former wife.[2]

- **Death of a Cohabitant:** In law, if a married person dies before his/her Will is made, that person died intestate. The surviving spouse will be able to inherit the late spouse's assets under intestacy laws in Singapore.[3] However, if a cohabitant dies without a Will, his/her partner does not inherit anything.

- **Tax Relief:** There is no tax relief available for cohabiting couples. However there are various types of tax relief married couples can apply for, or in some instances, receive automatically.

  1. Spouse Relief/Handicapped Spouse Relief[4] — Relief is conferred to encourage the formation of families in Singapore. From assessment year 2012, as long as the spouse did not have an annual income of more than $4,000 in the year before and the spouse was living with or supported by the taxpayer, he or she is able to benefit from a relief of $2,000 in his or her taxes submitted for the current year. In the case of a handicapped spouse, the income criterion does not apply and the amount of relief that may be claimed by such taxpayer is $5,500 effective assessment year 2015.[5] In this way, recognition is given to taxpayers that financially support their spouses.

  2. Parenthood Tax Rebate[6] — A rebate is provided to encourage married tax residents in Singapore to have more children. Under the scheme, a $5,000 rebate is given for children born or adopted on or after 01 January 2008 by Singapore tax residents who are "married,

---

[2]Matrimonial assets will be further discussed in Chapter 6.

[3]Intestate Succession Act (Cap. 146, 1985 Rev Ed) s. 7.

[4]More information can be found on the Inland Revenue Authority of Singapore website <http://www.iras.gov.sg> (accessed on 02 May 2013).

[5]Relief for handicapped spouse was $3,500 prior to Year of Assessment 2015: Inland Revenue of Authority Website (accessed 06 April 2016).

[6]*Ibid.*

divorced or widowed in the relevant year" of claim.[7] This rebate decreases the tax payable on their income and the amount can be split in whichever proportions the couple decides. It increases to a maximum of $20,000 per child after the family unit has had its third child. Also, any unused rebate can be set off against future income tax payable by the couple.

These are two common tax rebates currently not available to cohabiting couples.

- **Making Decisions on each other's behalf:** There is a lack of legal authority to make critical decisions for the other cohabitant under urgent circumstances. This can be overcome by the granting of a power of attorney or a lasting power of attorney by one cohabitant to the other.

- **Family Violence:** Where one spouse commits violence against the other, the victimised spouse can lodge a police report and obtain a Personal Protection Order from the court.[8] This is because Section 64 of the Women's Charter lists a spouse as a person protected from family violence. However, cohabitants cannot apply for a Personal Protection Order under the Women's Charter as they are not legal spouses.

  This does not mean that cohabitants do not have any legal recourse at all and are discriminated against by the law. Cohabitants continue to have access to the general criminal law provisions aimed at protecting people from acts of violence committed by strangers. Just as wilful contravention of the protection order constitutes a crime in the familial context,[9] so do acts of violence by a stranger, depending upon the specific circumstances.

- **Purchase of Property:** Housing & Development Board ("HDB") flats are subsidised public housing. Cohabiting couples who wish to purchase a HDB flat (as opposed to a private property) are restricted to purchasing resale HDB flats. They are not able to purchase a new HDB flat unless they intend to get married and fall under the Fiancé/Fiancée Scheme.

---

[7] The Parenthood Tax Rebate is not available in respect of a 1st child born or adopted before 01 January 2008.
[8] Women's Charter (Cap. 353, 2009 Rev Ed) s 65(1).
[9] *Id*, at s 65(8).

Most of the housing grants available to aid purchasers of HDB flats are for families. However, cohabiting couples may still be eligible for some housing grants if they fulfil the eligibility criteria to purchase a resale HDB flat under the Single Singapore Citizen Scheme or the Joint Singles Scheme.[10]

Of course, these grants apply only to public housing. A cohabiting couple who can afford private property may purchase their own property without a need to be engaged or married.

A cohabiting partner can be nominated as a beneficiary under the life insurance policy. A revocable nomination is made under the Insurance Act and the policy-holder can revoke his nomination anytime he or she feels like it. In contrast, when a married person buys an insurance policy for the benefit of his spouse (or children) with the intention to create a trust in favour of the spouse (or children), an irrevocable nomination is created. The death benefits of a life insurance policy in such a case do not form part of the policy-holder's estate to be divided upon his or her death. One advantage of this is that the funds remain safe from creditors. A revocation of a nomination with the intention to create a trust in favour of the spouse and/or child can only be done with the prior written consent of each nominee.

- **Lack of Legal Rights**: Married couples are conferred legal rights by virtue of their marital status. For example, when one spouse commits adultery, the other spouse may apply to the courts for a divorce to be granted. A cohabiting partner does not have the same legal recourse. Similarly, while the courts have the power to divide matrimonial assets belonging to married couples there is no such power over the assets of cohabiting couples.

A Final Note

The points above illustrate some of the practical issues a cohabiting couple faces.

---

[10] For more information on HDB flats, see <http://www.hdb.gov.sg>.

There are many factors that a couple thinking of cohabitating should consider. While such a "no strings attached" arrangement may appear to be advantageous, it should be borne in mind that that very fact may work against a cohabiting partner such as when the relationship ends after assets have been accumulated or where the relationship results in a child. As there are long-term implications for such a relationship, the decision to cohabit should not be taken lightly.

Chapter Two

The Second Step: Preparing for Marriage

The first bond of society is marriage.

— Cicero

Marriage is more than a choice. It is a public declaration of love and commitment made by the couple, a coming together of both families, friends and also a promise that is made before God[1] and the community.

Yet, a different picture of marriage is often painted in popular culture. In today's world of "Hollywood Marriages"[2] where divorces and breakups are common, the sanctity of marriage is a topic more relevant than ever before. Frequent encounters with marriages that end in divorces could be an unfortunate explanation why many singles today choose to view marriage with such apprehension and in some extreme cases abhorrence.

---

[1] For Roman Catholics, marriage is known as the "Holy Estate of Matrimony". Couples who believe in God have an added anchor that helps them through challenging times.

[2] Hollywood stars and celebrities are known to have marriages as short as 72 days and 55 hours.

This chapter hopes to bring you back to the core of marriage to examine what the institution of marriage entails for you in the eyes of the law. The general legal requirements of marriage and the enforceability of the increasing use of prenuptial agreements will also be discussed. This will hopefully help the couple make an informed choice as this next step in the relationship is considered.

WHAT IS MARRIAGE

History of Marriage

The origins of marriage remain a mystery. Many anthropologists believe that the concept of marriage began about 4,000 years ago.[3] Before then, families consisted of loosely organised groups of roughly thirty people. It was only when agrarian civilisations developed the concept of companionship, that the idea of marriage was born.[4] Over subsequent centuries, marriage evolved into a widespread institution embraced by ancient civilisations.[5] Marriage at that time was used as a currency to provide economic and social stability. In some cases, marriages were conducted to protect a family's bloodline. Then, the ideology of gender equality was not widely accepted and women were often viewed as chattels of their husbands.

The Political Battle[6]

The rights a woman had in nineteenth century England were dependent upon her marital status. A married woman could not own any property,

---

[3] One possible reason for believing so is the existence of the Code of Hammurabi which is nearly 4,000 years old. The Code governs marriage and family relations.

[4] Agrarian societies are societies that depend on farming as their main means of subsistence.

[5] See for example marriages in ancient Greece, <www.historylink101.com/2/greece3/marriage.htm>.

[6] Reproduced for illustrative purposes only and does not necessarily reflect the view of the author.

including herself. Instead, her husband owned her as his property. Hence in law, any property or goods a married woman brought to the marriage, including inherited land and monies, belonged to her husband.

In 1855, Caroline Norton, a feminist writer and reformer, wrote a letter to the Queen, reviewing the position of married women in the early nineteenth century.[7] Some of her observations are listed below:

1. A married woman has no legal personality;
2. A married woman cannot make a Will, the law gives what she has to her husband despite her wishes or his behavior;
3. A wife cannot legally claim her own earnings;
4. If the wife is guilty of infidelity, her husband may divorce her but she cannot divorce him, no matter how profligate he may be;

In short, a wife held no right to anything that was his; whereas as her husband, he had the right to all that was hers.

The feminist movement, beginning in the late eighteenth century, rallied against this highly unequal status of women. In 1870, a significant piece of legislation was passed in the United Kingdom to work towards equalising the rights and elevating the status of married women.[8]

Fortunately for women, the concept of marriage nowadays revolves around the notion of personal autonomy.[9] Marriage is more about an individual being given the freedom to fulfill his/her deepest needs of companionship with his/her loved one to cherish until death. It is no longer an agreement that benefits the male but allows both husband and wife to grow, learn and rely on each other in a more balanced and complementary way.

---

[7]*A Letter to the Queen on Lord Chancellor Cranworth's Marriage and Divorce Bill* by the Hon. Mrs. Norton, Caroline Sheridan, "Only a Woman's Hair", Thackeray's Lecture on Swift. London: Longman, Brown, Green and Longmans, 1855.

[8]The English legislation mentioned here refers to the Married Women's Property Act 1870.

[9]Mainly because jobs and education have empowered women to have autonomy such that Asian women are marrying later. See <http//www.economist.com/node/21526329>.

Definition of Marriage in Singapore

While the Women's Charter does not expressly define the term "marriage", it rejects the possibility of a legally recognised polygamous marriage.[10] Singapore law defines a monogamous marriage as a voluntary union of one man and one woman to the exclusion of all others.[11]

Singapore does not recognise same-sex marriages. Under the Women's Charter, marriage can only be a union of one man and one woman.

What about Men and Children?

The Women's Charter provides not only for the protection of women, and for divorce and ancillary matters, it actually covers family law in Singapore. In fact, the Association of Women for Action and Research (AWARE) petitioned in 2011 to change the name of the Women's Charter to the Family Charter "on the basis that the latter would better reflect the contents of the legislation as well as be more gender neutral".[12]

Marriage vows mention love, honour, care and fidelity as key tenets of the legal union between a man and a woman. "Till death do us part" are the famous words voiced in many a movie and constantly serve to remind us of the length of the contract one "signs" when one says "I do". It is therefore important that the couple keep these precepts in mind as they think of and plan their momentous day.

---

[10]Women's Charter (Cap. 353, 2009 Rev Ed) s 4(3).

[11]Interpretation Act (Cap. 1, 2002 Rev Ed) s 2; *Id*, at s 12.

[12]More information can be found on the website of Association of Women for Action and Research (AWARE). See also the lively discussion in Parliament on Women's Charter (Review) between Mr Charles Chong and Mr Chan Soo Sen (then Minister of State for Community Development and Sports) on amending the title of the Women's Charter to "Family Charter". Singapore Parliament Reports: Women's Charter (Review) 1st October 2002, column 1094–1095.

Marriage vows are statements personal to the couple. Both parties may choose to adopt the standard vows, amend them as they wish or otherwise write their own from scratch.

PRENUPTIAL AGREEMENTS

Section 46(1) of the Women's Charter treats marital partners as equal partners in a co-operative effort. The Court[13] has noted that the just and equitable distribution provision under the Women's Charter recognises a marriage as an equal co-operative partnership of efforts. The contributions of each partner (both financial and non-financial) in the marriage would be translated into economic assets for distribution when the marriage breaks up. Therefore, if we consider a marriage as a quasi-economic partnership, the partners themselves would be the best people to decide how to divide their assets in the event of a breakdown.[14] Some would argue that one way to achieve this is to enable enforcement of agreements made by the partners when they first entered into the partnerships, which, in the marital context, is the prenuptial agreement. Objectors would argue that it is not right for parties to be planning for a breakup even before the marriage has taken place. Also, because marriage brings with it conjugal duties and responsibilities which include physical intimacy, child bearing and child raising, many would find it repugnant and demeaning to even consider a prenuptial agreement.

What is a Prenuptial Agreement?

A prenuptial agreement is basically a written agreement that seeks to govern various aspects of a married life. It may include both financial and non-financial obligations. In Singapore, prenuptial agreements are generally not directly enforceable. In general, the court is less willing to enforce any agreement which seeks to pre-determine the amount of maintenance for one's

---

[13]NK v. NL [2007] SGCA 35 at [20].

[14]*Miller v Miller* [2006] UKHL 24 at [16]; *McFarlane v; McFarlane* [2006] 2 AC 618 at pp 632–633 per Lord Nicholls of Birkenhead, referring to *R v R* [1992] 1 AC 599 at p 617, that "the husband and wife are now for all practical purposes equal partners in marriage."

spouse (and children), and custody of the children. This is because these issues directly involve the welfare of individual persons. Any change in circumstances could impact them adversely. Further, the paramount consideration for the court is children's issues such as custody and maintenance. However, the court seems increasingly more willing to consider prenuptial agreements in the context of division of matrimonial assets.[15] Therefore the issue of division of assets in a prenuptial agreement will be the focus of our subsequent discussion.

Prenuptial agreements often provide for financial arrangements such as:

- The amount of maintenance the wife should receive during the marriage and
- How the matrimonial assets should be divided should the marriage break down

Non-financial provisions in prenuptial agreements are usually treated as merely morally binding. Examples are:

- Where the couple should live and
- The number of children to have

Prenuptial Agreements in the Context of Divorce Law

Since most prenuptial agreements are intended to have effect only in a divorce, it is important to understand the prevailing law in Singapore with regard to the division of matrimonial assets. This will be discussed in detail in Chapter 6. In the event of a divorce, the Court is empowered under Section 112 of the Women's Charter, 'to order the division between the parties of any matrimonial assets … in such proportions as the court thinks just and equitable'. The rationale is that both spouses have played a part whether by financial or non-financial means and contributed to the acquisition of matrimonial assets.

---

[15]*TQ v TR* [2009] SGCA 6.

The Law Governing Prenuptial Agreements

Prenuptial agreements usually relate to financial matters. They focus on property and maintenance after the marriage ends. Marriage is a contract in the sense that both parties must agree to enter into it and after that both are bound by its legal consequences. A central purpose of many prenuptial agreements is to alter the status quo that imposes a default formula for spousal rights. By entering into a prenuptial agreement, a couple hopes to structure their finances according to a pre-determined plan.

Although a prenuptial agreement is not generally enforceable in Singapore, a prenuptial agreement is one of the factors that the Court may consider when dividing matrimonial assets. In *TQ v TR*,[16] the Court of Appeal followed the following principles of law before determining whether a prenuptial agreement may be considered:

1. The prenuptial agreement must not be inherently unlawful or against public policy;[17]
2. It must have the elements required for a contract i.e. offer and acceptance and there must be an absence of vitiating factors such as misrepresentation, mistake, undue influence, duress, unconscionability, as well as illegality and public policy;[18]
3. A prenuptial agreement is always subject to scrutiny by the court[19] which will exercise judicial discretion in a just and equitable manner within the laws of division of matrimonial assets and maintenance upon divorce;[20] and
4. The court determines the weight that is to be given to the prenuptial agreement pertaining to the division of matrimonial assets and depending on the facts of the case, the court may accord a significant (even conclusive) weight to the agreement (it does not matter whether the agreement has any foreign element or not).[21]

---

[16] *Ibid*.

[17] *Id*, at [53].

[18] *Id*, at [94]–[100].

[19] *Id*, at [103]–[104].

[20] See Leong Wai Kum, *Prenuptial Agreement on Division of Matrimonial Assets Subject to Court Scrutiny*, [2009] SJLS 211 at 225.

[21] *Supra*, n 15, at [103].

A prenuptial agreement in Singapore is governed both by statute law (i.e. the Women's Charter) on the one hand and common law on the other. Where the Women's Charter expressly covers prenuptial agreements, it would prevail. Where the Women's Charter is silent, the prenuptial agreement would be governed by common law.[22]

Do you need a Prenuptial Agreement?

Not every couple needs a prenuptial agreement. Prenuptial agreements usually come into play when there is a disparity in the wealth of the future spouses or their families. Younger partners entering into their first marriage are often less likely to be unequally paired. They may start with little money or no savings which makes for an equal pairing from the outset, sharing their income as they earn it. However, second or later life marriages or couples who have greater gaps in age may encounter the dilemma of whether to have a prenuptial agreement. They may have a need to protect their assets for their children from former marriages or simply wish to prevent a recurrence of the bitterness from a previous divorce.[23]

Parties may also use prenuptial agreements as an instrument to safeguard family wealth or business built up by past generations from disputes that may potentially arise upon death or divorce.[24] Other likely candidates for prenuptial agreements include two-income families who prioritise a career for both partners (they are not prepared to give half of their income and property to a divorced spouse who refuses to work or prefers to enjoy life instead of a lucrative but stressful job), couples comprising spouses of different nationalities, couples who buy a home before marrying or in which one pays for the other's education, and couples where one spouse has incurred a lot of debt.

Since a marriage is usually governed by a statute and the court interprets these statutes based on the perception of a typical couple, it is costly to be

---

[22]*Id*, at [50] and [102].

[23]Allison A Marston, "Planning for Love: the Politics of Prenuptial Agreements" (1997) 49 Stan L Rev 887 at 889.

[24]See for example *Granatino v Radmacher* [2010] UKSC 42 where the parents of the German Heiress Radmacher pressed their daughter to enter into a prenuptial agreement with her future husband before transferring substantial amount of assets to her.

different. For example, traditional divorce law has developed based on cases where the families arise from first marriages. As a result the traditional law has not developed to balance the claims of a family from a second marriage against the needs of the family from the first marriage.

It seems that there could be an increasing willingness by the court to let parties contract the terms of their marriage or separation.[25] An academic has said that the Court of Appeal decision in *TQ v TR* is a progressive step for Singapore in supporting private ordering.[26] The Court should both encourage private settlements and ensure that the parties are treated fairly. Awareness of the court's control would encourage parties to enter into fair agreements. The courts will tend to give effect to agreements that are not exceptionally unfair. Overtime, precedents will be developed which will help to clarify the law.

Should you sign a Prenuptial Agreement?

This is a tough question to answer because it would ultimately depend on the circumstances and subjective preferences of the parties. However, it is important to keep an open mind when you are deciding whether or not to sign a prenuptial agreement. Considering that in general men are marrying later compared to women[27] and men have greater earning power than women,[28]

---

[25] See for example *Tan Siew Eng @ Tan Siew Eng Irene (m.w) v Ng Meng Hin* [2003] SLR 474 where the High Court made an order based on the terms of the Settlement Agreement which had been extensively negotiated by the parties. It was subsequently repudiated. Even so, the agreement still gave the best indication of what was a just and equitable division particularly where there was a lack of full disclosure of assets, which made the task of division extremely difficult for the court.

[26] Debbie Ong Siew Ling, "Prenuptial Agreements and Foreign Matrimonial Agreements: *TQ v TK*" (2007) SAcLJ 397 at [36]. See also the majority decision in *Granatino* where the Supreme Court in England concluded that there were no factors which rendered it unfair to hold the husband to the pre-nuptial agreement.

[27] The State of the Family Report 2011 issued by National Family Council stated that the median age at first marriage for men is 30.0 in 2010 while the median age at first marriage for women is 27.7 in 2010. The report was last accessed on 7 February 2014 at <http://www.nfc.org.sg/pdf/Requestor_SOFR%202011%20Cicada%20v8%20Final.pdf> but is no longer active. The National Family Council has since been renamed "Families for Life".

[28] See Ministry of Man Power (2011), *Report on Wages in Singapore*. The survey also indicated that men are consistently paid higher than women in Singapore, regardless of their education level.

it is often the case that the wife-to-be is the one being asked to sign the prenuptial agreement.

Opponents of prenuptial agreements often base their objections on the ground that women are socially and psychologically disadvantaged in negotiations as they have a greater "distaste for disagreement" and a stronger "taste for cooperation".[29] The woman is usually more emotionally involved and reluctant to question the man's motives or purposes. She wants to get married and does not contemplate the agreement being tested in a divorce court. An author has also argued that women are poorer negotiators than men because of a power imbalance deriving from women's greater dedication to family life.[30]

There are two responses to the above charges: First, it is not in every society that women can be said to be unfairly disadvantaged as far as marriage is concerned. It all depends on the progress of gender equalisation in that particular society. Hence, in Singapore, a society characterised by high workforce participation rate (56.5% in 2010) and relatively advanced educational levels among women (93.8% literacy rate among women and over half of entering students in universities were female),[31] it is doubtful whether this assumption of gender inequality that affect women's bargaining power to enter a marriage holds true since education and jobs have been described as the two forces giving women more autonomy.[32] Education changes women's expectations of their partners and having a job gives a woman more options including not having a husband who does not match with her expectation.[33]

Nowadays, more women can contribute financially to the marriage because of better education and increased economic participation which often leads to later marriages. It is not too far-fetched to suggest that some

---

[29] Carol M. Rose, Women and Property: Gaining and Losing Ground, 78 Va. L. Rev. 421, 423 (1992).

[30] See Mary Becker, Problems with the Privatization of Heterosexuality, 73 Denv. U. L. Rev. 1169, 1172 (1996).

[31] See <http://www.un.org/News/Press/docs/2011/wom1875.doc.htm>. According to the report, Singapore is also placed ten out of 138 countries on the United Nations Gender Inequality Index.

[32] See The flight from marriage, at <http://www.economist.com/node/21526329>.

[33] This also partially explains low birth rate in Singapore. Latest Statistics shows that Singapore has a high proportion of women aged 30–34 who remain single at 25% in 2010.

women might use prenuptial agreements to protect their pre-marital assets.[34] One journalist believes that "creating a good prenuptial agreement is one of the most romantic and loving things a person can do for their intended". At the end of the day a prenuptial agreement is "a promise to treat each other with respect even when you've lost that loving feeling".[35]

Foreign Prenuptial Agreements

Foreign prenuptial agreements are agreements made by foreign nationals in a foreign country. As compared to local prenuptial agreements, the court seems to have given foreign prenuptial agreements greater weight.[36]

It was held by the court that "if a prenuptial agreement is entered into by foreign nationals and governed by (as well as valid according to) a foreign law (assuming that the foreign law is not repugnant to the public policy of Singapore), there is no reason in principle why the court should not accord significant (even critical) weight to the terms of the agreement." Unlike local prenuptial agreements, there is no requirement that it should fulfill the requirements of contract law in Singapore.[37]

Ultimately, the courts decide on whether to give effect to the prenuptial agreement. Whether or not it wishes to give weight to the whole agreement or to even consider the agreement depends on the facts of the specific case.

Travelling the World Together [38]

A foreign couple met in the United Kingdom and fell in love. They got married in the Netherlands. Prior to their marriage, they signed a

---

[34]This is reflected in the law in Singapore, for example, in the presumption of gift of property transferred from husband to his wife and not vice versa. See also Singapore Legislative Assembly Debates, Women's Charter (Review), 10 January 2002, where it was not accepted (at that time) that there could be maintenance for men even though 1800 households had male homemakers.

[35]Naomi Alderman, "Prenups: To have and hold on to", The Daily Mail, 1 August 2009 <http://www.dailymail.co.uk/home/you/article-1203265/To-hold-to.html> (accessed 6 December 2016).

[36]*Supra* n 15.

[37]*Ibid.*

[38]*Ibid.*

prenuptial agreement to keep their assets separate during the marriage. This agreement was prepared by a Dutch civil law Notary and executed according to Dutch law. After 6 years of marriage they decided to settle in the shores of Singapore. Unfortunately, very soon after their move to Singapore, their marriage deteriorated. A divorce application was filed and the husband attempted to enforce their Dutch prenuptial agreement.

The local courts decided that the foreign prenuptial agreement was valid in Singapore as it was amongst others: (1) valid under foreign law, in this case, Dutch law, and (2) did not go against the grain of s 112 of the Women's Charter and common law, and the best interests of the children. As a result, the husband won his case and the court did not have to order a division of the couple's assets post-divorce since their assets were already kept separate.

In conclusion, the courts will consider agreements made between parties in reaching its decision for the division of matrimonial assets. However the actual weight to be accorded depends on the precise circumstances and facts before the court. Therefore, prenuptial agreements are not entirely a waste because the courts may still give the agreement some weight in reaching their decisions.

Are Marriage Vows Oral Contracts?

Marriage vows, as earlier discussed, underscore the sanctity of the marriage as well as its longevity. Many take its content as reminders of their commitment to each other. But do vows legally bind both man and wife?

This seemingly simple question holds greater implications than meets the eye. What happens to the legality of your marriage should a licence not be issued but where vows have already been exchanged? Where marriage vows have been written from scratch, will both you and your spouse be able to hold your vows as an oral contract and enforce it in court? If vows were legally enforceable, would we all have to ensure the absence of loopholes in this presumably romantic exchange of promises? The inconvenience this would cause for the drafting of your marriage vows may be good business for lawyers but may be unwarranted for you.

Do marriage vows amount to an oral contract? Offer and acceptance can be found in the exchange of "I do" at the end of marriage vows. With them being said in the presence of witnesses, there is usually an intention of permanence and perhaps the intention of both parties to create legal relations, the latter being a prerequisite to the finding of a valid contract under law. In addition, can it also be said that it is also a tenable proposition that consideration has been provided by the couple? (Consideration is the giving of a promise flowing from one party to the other.) Because the law of contract has evolved to allow for consideration as small as a peppercorn,[39] can it be argued that, marriage vows followed by the exchange of rings satisfy the element of consideration?

As seen above, marital agreements are generally not enforceable in courts. Instead, the exchange may only give rise to social or moral obligations.

Marriage is a risky gamble of sorts. Yet billions of people around the world brave the risks and marry. That is because there is something beautiful about the institution of marriage, about the union between two people in love, a relationship that should withstand the ups and downs of life, in sickness and in health. There is something wonderful about embarking on an unknown journey with the person you truly care for and exploring the many different roles one can take on in a relationship. Your partner will be your best friend, your lover, your soul mate, your psychoanalyst, your life coach and maybe sometimes your enemy. A prenuptial agreement may reduce the risk of the unexpected, but the question that ought to be asked is, "At what cost?"

WHAT MAKES A VALID MARRIAGE?

A valid marriage will continue until the death of either spouse or until it is dissolved by an order or declaration by the courts. Before getting married, each party has to consider the consequences as life-long and be prepared for a personal change. The law also recognises this life-long commitment and seeks to create a distinction between the legal rights of two singles living together and a married couple. Hence the law sets a few minimum

---

[39] *Chappell & Co Ltd & Anor v Nestle Co Ltd & Anor* [1960] 1 AC 87.

requirements that both parties must satisfy before their marriage can be considered legal and official.

If any of these requirements is not met, a marriage may be considered void or voidable. When a marriage is declared void, this means that in the eyes of the law, it is as though the marriage never existed due to the element of unlawfulness or invalidity. When a marriage is voidable (i.e. a legal marriage which can be cancelled by the court if contested by one of the parties) i.e. suffering a less grievous flaw as opposed to a void marriage that has been described as suffering a more grievous flaw, parties may choose to obtain a judgement of nullity and have the marriage declared void.[40]

When Your Heart Doesn't Go On[41]

In 2007 in the United States of America, a wife sued her husband for divorce after two decades of marriage. This was no ordinary divorce hearing. The husband claimed in his defence that when his heart temporarily stopped in June 2004, his marriage was dissolved. This was in accordance with the Connecticut laws which at that time stated that a marriage is dissolved by the death of one of the parties.

Unfortunately for him, his motion failed in court. The judge held that on the facts of the case, there was no irreversible cessation of all vital functions including the brain. Since his death was not permanent and neither was it irreversible, his defence was denied.

Eligibility to Marry

Before marrying, you and your intended other half must ensure that you satisfy the following legal requirements in order for the marriage to be valid, and not void or voidable:

---

[40]See Leong Wai Kum, Elements of Family Law in Singapore, (LexisNexis 2013, 2nd Ed) at pp 50, 51, & 63.
[41]Thomas B. Scheffey, "A Husband with a Death Wish" (2008) Connecticut Law Tribune. This story is reproduced for illustrative purposes only.

(a) **Both you and your spouse-to-be must be at least 18 years old:**[42]
If a person is below 18 years old, a Special Marriage License must be obtained from the Minister of Social and Family Development[43] before the marriage is legal.[44] In addition, if a party is under 21 years old i.e. a minor, his or her parent or guardian must give consent in writing before a marriage license is issued.[45] Where consent has been refused in any of the cases, the party concerned may apply for consent from the High Court.

(b) **Both you and your spouse-to-be cannot be too closely related to each other:**[46] This includes all incestuous relationships including marrying your own parents or grandparents, for example.[47]

The Case of Accidental Incest [48]

In 2008, during the British parliamentary debate regarding a child's right to access information about his or her biological parents, Lord Alton revealed a cruel but true story of 'accidental incest'.

Told by a High Court judge who had presided over the case, the story involved a pair of twins who had been separated at birth and adopted by different families. However, years later, the twins met by pure coincidence and felt an 'inevitable attraction' towards each other. Not knowing their true biological relationship, they got married. Yet, their happiness was short-lived as the marriage was annulled by the court when the truth was later revealed that there existed a prohibited degree of consanguinity between them.

---

[42] *Supra* n 10, at s 9.

[43] More elaboration can be found on the Ministry of Social and Family Development website <http://app.msf.gov.sg/ResearchRoom/ResearchStatistics/SpecialMarriageLicense> (accessed on 13 Jan 2014).

[44] *Supra* n 10, at ss 9 & 21(2).

[45] *Id*, at s 13 and 17.

[46] *Id*, at s 10.

[47] A detailed list of prohibited relationships can be found on the Registry of Marriages' website <http://app.rom.gov.sg/reg_info/rom_other.asp> (accessed 13 Jan 2014).

[48] Fiona Barton, "Shock for the Married Couple who Discovered They are Twins Separated at Birth" Mail Online (11 January 2008). See also <www.dailymail.co.uk/news/article-507588>.

(c) **Both you and your spouse-to-be must be unmarried:**[49] Polygamous marriages for non-Muslims are not recognised by the Women's
Charter.[50] Hence under the Women's Charter any marriage with a person
already married is void even if all other marriage procedures under any
law, religion, custom or usage anywhere are followed and even if the first
marriage was soleminised in a different country.

Double Trouble[51]

T met a 26-year-old woman while he was working in Indonesia in 2005.
Within months, they were married and the marriage was registered in
Singapore. However, in September, it was revealed that T was already
married for 23 years in Johor Bahru, Malaysia. He even had 4 children
from the prior marriage, but had kept it a secret from his second wife.

The truth came out when his first wife suspected him of infidelity and
ran a check on the Registry of Marriages only to find his second marriage
registered in Singapore. She then lodged a police report and T was
charged and convicted of committing bigamy. Not only was his second
marriage in Singapore held to be null and void, he was also sentenced to
5 months' imprisonment.[52]

(d) **You and your spouse-to-be cannot be of the same gender:**[53]
    This is because only heterosexual marriages are recognised in Singapore.

---

[49]*Supra* n 10, at s 5 read with s 11.

[50]*Id*, at s 4. 15 September 1961 marked the date when the Registry of Marriages
was set up to register and solemnize civil marriages under the Women's Charter
and polygamy for non-Muslims was abolished. However, customary marriages entered
into before 2nd June 1967 were recognized as valid marriages. From 2nd June
1967, marriages solemnized in Singapore are only recognized as valid marriages if
they are in accordance with the Women's Charter. See <http://www.app.rom.gov.sg/
about_rom/romabout.asp>.

[51]*Public Prosecutor v Tan Ser Ping* [2006] SGDC 95.

[52]Penal Code (Cap. 224, 2008 Rev Ed) s 494.

[53]*Supra* n 10, at s 12.

A discussion on the definition of marriage is found earlier in the chapter but is generally straightforward. It becomes slightly more confusing if the marriage involves a hermaphrodite or transgender man or woman. However, the law states that the gender of any given person is determined by what is stated in his or her identity card at the time of marriage and not by the birth certificate.[54] Hence if a hermaphrodite or transgender man or woman has changed his or her gender on his or her identity card, the marriage will be valid.

I Didn't Know I Married a Woman[55]

On one fine day in the year 1953, a baby girl was born. However, at the age of 35, this girl underwent a sex reassignment procedure and changed her name to Eric. Eric's identity card was amended to reflect that she was male. Three years later, Eric got married. After a prolonged period of failing to consummate their marriage, Eric finally admitted to his wife that he was a transsexual. She was angry and felt tricked. She tried to annul the marriage on the basis that Eric was biologically a female and a marriage between two females was impossible in law since they were unable to consummate the marriage.

The court held that a person's gender is determined biologically. It did not matter that Eric had undergone sex-change surgery and was psychologically male. It also did not matter that he was recognised as a male on his identity card. Thus, their marriage was declared void.

A Change in the Law:

The case above resulted in a momentous change in the Women's Charter in 1996. Hence, under today's law, the marriage between Eric and his wife would be a legal marriage as the sex reassignment procedure would render Eric a male and Eric's sex would be determined by that stated in his identity card.

---

[54]*Id*, at s 12(3)(a).
[55]*Lim Ying v Hiok Kian Ming Eric* [1991] 2 SLR(R) 525.

(e) **Both you and your spouse-to-be are not Muslims**: The Women's Charter does not apply to Muslim marriages. For Muslims, reference may be made to the Administration of Muslim Law Act and/or the Syariah Court for more information on the validity of a Muslim marriage.[56]

(f) **Both you and your spouse-to-be must follow marriage rules of solemnization:** The couple must solemnize the marriage that is authorised by a valid marriage licence and the solemnization must be performed by a licensed marriage official.

Where any of these requirements in "examples" (a)–(f) above is not met, the marriage will be declared void and the effect is the same as if the marriage had not taken place. However, whether declared void or otherwise, the fact that a marriage was registered will still be recorded in the Registry of Marriages.

The points below concern some grounds on which a marriage may be considered voidable. An annulment made on the ground of a voidable marriage operates like a divorce in that it terminates a marriage. However, unlike a divorce, an annulled marriage returns the couple to their prior status before the marriage.

Marry with Valid Consent

Marriage is similar to a contract. Hence, the law encourages parties to marry willingly and on their own volition. In the extreme, agreeing to marry a person under pressure from your parents or anyone else may be considered duress. In such cases where a person marries without valid consent, that marriage may be voidable.

When Saying "I Do" Means Something Else[57]

G was a 20-year-old female (not a full fledged adult) who lived with her parents and earned $500 a month. Her parents arranged for a

---

[56]*Supra*, n 10, at s 105(A).

[57]*Geetha d/o Mundri v Arivananthan s/o Retnam* [1992] 1 SLR(R) 326; [1992] 2 SLR 422.

matchmaker to introduce a husband for G to marry. They gave consent for her to marry and gave notice of marriage. When she saw her potential husband, G told her family members that she did not want to marry him. For the next 12 days, she was slapped, insulted and repeatedly scolded for refusing to register the marriage. G eventually gave in and said "I do". The married couple never lived together and G was not happy with the marriage.

About 6 months later and 2 days after G turned 21, G applied for the marriage to be annulled. She succeeded as the court decided that G had been in an inescapable dilemma when she said "I do". She had only 2 choices under duress: to marry the man or face continued abuse at home. Hence, her consent was not valid and the marriage was annulled, as the Court held that free consent of the person who is marrying must be obtained.

Another situation where consent can be found to be invalid is where either spouse had agreed to marry the other under a mistaken belief. There is sparse legal authority on what amounts to a mistake in case of marriage. A straight-forward example could be mistakes relating to a person's identity. However, this is no easy task to prove, because of the difficulty in convincing the court that there was a mistake as to a person's identity. The court will not allow the marriage to be voidable if there was a mistake as to a person's attributes.[58]

As the consequences of holding a marriage voidable (or void) are grave, the courts are slow to make such findings. For example, one party's motive in consenting to marriage cannot be used to argue that he or she entered into the marriage under a mistake of his or her spouse's intentions.

Motives For A Marriage Not Considered By The Court

In *Tan Ah Thee and another v Lim Soo Foong*,[59] the deceased had been married twice during his lifetime, first to one Mdm K and after her death

---

[58]*Supra* n 41, at p 74.
[59][2009] SGHC 101.

to the defendant. The plaintiffs were children of Mdm K. The deceased's relationship with the defendant actually began during his marriage with Mdm K and, out of this extramarital relationship, a son, TGC, was born. After Mdm K's death, the deceased publicly acknowledged his relationships with the defendant and TGC and, on 11 March 1996, a marriage was solemnized between the deceased and Mdm Lim. After the deceased's death, the High Court set aside his last will (a will is revoked by a subsequent marriage) and ordered that his estate be distributed in accordance with the provisions of the Intestate Succession Act (Cap 146, 1985 Rev Ed), thereby, entitling the defendant as the spouse of the deceased, to one-half of the deceased's estate.

Subsequently, the plaintiffs, as administrators of the deceased estate, sought a declaration that the marriage between the deceased and Mdm Lim was null and void on the ground that it was a sham marriage, registered solely or predominantly to revoke the will made by the deceased prior to marriage. This is because at the time of the marriage the deceased was 81 years old, wheelchair bound and suffering from Parkinson's disease. The plaintiffs claimed that the marriage was procured by the actual or presumed undue influence of the defendant over the deceased. The Court refused to grant the declaration sought by the plaintiffs and held that the law desisted from identifying what the proper motives of marriage were and did not allow the parties' private motives to undermine the validity of marriage.

A last situation where a lack of valid consent to a marriage can be found is where the spouse is able to establish in court that either party was at the time when consent was given, suffering from a mental disorder.[60] The giving of consent while one or both parties is not in a lucid state is not a giving of valid consent. The term "mental disorder" is defined in the Mental Health (Care and Treatment) Act as any mental illness or any other disorder or disability of the mind.[61]

---

[60]*Supra* n 10, at s 106(d).
[61]Mental Health (Care and Treatment) Act (Cap 178A, 2012 Rev Ed) s 2(1).

Be Truthful

One way to foster trust between the couple is for both parties to be forthcoming about any critical information which may affect the marital relationship. The type of information that should be told is mostly left to one's discretion. However, at the bare minimum, there are three types of information which must be disclosed. Disclosure may not save the situation, but a failure to do so could cause the marriage to be annulled.

- **Contagious Sexually-Transmitted Disease (STD):** A person suffering from a contagious venereal disease[62] must inform a potential spouse of his or her health condition before the marriage.[63]

  In fact, Singapore makes it a crime to transmit AIDS or the HIV infection to another knowingly. This would include spousal infections where an HIV carrier chooses to have sexual intercourse, without informing his or her partner of the risk of transmission of AIDS or HIV infection and obtaining his or her voluntary acceptance of such risk despite being aware of the other's medical condition. Anyone who is guilty of this crime could be fined up to $50,000 or imprisoned for up to 10 years or both.[64]

- **Mental Disorders:** Any party who is suffering from a mental disorder and knows of it, should disclose this to his or her potential spouse.[65]

  However, the "mental disorder" must be of a kind or of the extent that makes the sufferer unfit for marriage such that the sufferer is incapable of understanding the rigours of marriage. Only then can the marriage be annulled on this ground.

- **Pregnancy:** A woman who is pregnant by anyone other than her fiancé at the time of the marriage should inform her fiancé of this fact.[66]

---

[62]A venereal disease is a disease transmitted by sexual contact. This is also known as STDs and includes chlamydia, gonorrhoea and syphilis.

[63]*Supra* n 10, at s 106(e).

[64]Infectious Diseases Act (Cap. 137, 2003 Rev Ed) s 23(3).

[65]*Supra* n 62.

[66]*Supra* n 10, at s 106(f).

If any of the above categories of information is not told to your spouse, the marriage can be voidable and your spouse who was kept in the dark can choose to obtain a judgment of nullity or have the marriage declared void.

> ### The Deadly Lie[67]
>
> A 27-year-old former civil engineer was convicted under the Infectious Diseases Act.[68] He claimed that he did not intend to harm the victim, but hid the truth out of "self-protection" for fear that his social circle would abandon him. Not once did he tell the truth of his disease.
>
> The court chided him for being selfish and found him guilty, sentencing him to 18 months of jail. Sadly, his victim was later found to be HIV positive.

The above categories of information are merely the minimum that the law requires of each party. It certainly does not reflect the extent of information which could be and perhaps should be communicated between you and your intended spouse. Understandably, couples often find it awkward to talk about these issues and choose to sweep them under the carpet.

Other grounds that could make a marriage voidable include, amongst others, non-consummation due to incapacity of either party and the wilful refusal of the Defendant to consummate the marriage.[69]

PRE-MARITAL DISCLOSURE

It is well understood that trust is one of the basic building blocks of a healthy relationship. In the section above, we discussed the building blocks the law has set in place. However, to build a relationship of trust, parties ought to be truthful to one another and build on the basic foundation set by law. This

---

[67]*Man gets 18 months' Jail for not Disclosing HIV Status before Sex*, Channel News Asia, 18 January 2012. <http://news.asiaone.com/News/AsiaOne+News/Crime/Story/A1Story 20120118-322660.html>.
[68]*Supra* n 65.
[69]*Supra* n 10, at ss 106(a) & (b).

must begin even before marriage and should go above and beyond the bare minimum necessitated by law.

Overcome the Awkwardness

While there is no legal duty to disclose certain categories of information to your future spouse, some information may become a stain on the relationship if it is revealed too late. The spouse who was kept in the dark may feel hoodwinked into the marriage and in that sense, the marriage would be built on a shaky foundation. A sense of betrayal or deceit could then lead to a quick slide down the slippery road to divorce. Of course, this depends on the parties' personalities and response to this situation. That is why you and your partner are encouraged to overcome any awkwardness and discuss these issues before marriage.

A Legal Argument

A marriage has been likened to a lifelong contract. So, with the coveted signature able to bind a party to all terms and conditions, no matter how onerous, how does the sanctity of marriage fare when contrasted with contract law?

A contract can be rescinded by misrepresentation. This means that parties to the contract are put back in their original legal positions as if no contract had been made in the first place. Silence or non-disclosure may not necessarily constitute a representation, but if each party makes a positive but incomplete disclosure and this omission distorts the truth to the extent that a falsehood is created, it may amount to a misrepresentation. Similarly, where he or she then fails to correct a representation that subsequently becomes incorrect due to a material change in circumstances, this may be considered a misrepresentation.[70]

Love is an intangible notion that should cover all aspects of a person, including traits that inspire and those that may be barely tolerable. The legal question would be whether all characteristics and actions of a person should then be taken to be enough to be actionable in court, seeing that each aspect of a person amounts to a fact that induced the party into signing a contract of marriage with him or her.

---

[70]*With v O'Flannagan* [1936] Ch 575.

What if your spouse stashes away a secret bundle of cash without telling you? And what if you or your partner hides his or her ethnic ancestry or health history? Or the accuracy of his or her bank balance by bringing you on dates to taste the finer things in life that you may so deserve, before the veil is lifted to reveal a married future solely reliant on your pay cheque or borrowings? The risk of damaging or hurting the relationship then becomes very real.

As mentioned earlier, the law makes no such legal obligation on either party. Rather, the relevant question would be whether such a misrepresentation should amount to deception and correspondingly, a lack of valid consent that would make a marriage voidable.

The realisation of the corresponding ripples in contract law should alert potential spouses to the significance of pre-marital disclosure. Having this in mind, it is clear that letting a partner know of the skeletons in the closet, of the habits and "at-home behaviour" is not something to be taken lightly. Accountability is what one can expect to receive and give in a committed relationship. Pre-marital disclosure is a reasonable method of answering to that sense of accountability.

What can be Done

It is therefore prudent for couples to find out more about each other before they commit themselves to marriage. Other questions that a couple may want to ask include those questions that relate to either party's religious and political affiliations, expectations of how future leisure time will be spent, ability and willingness to bear children, communication and conflict management methods.

Honey, Shall We Have A Little Chat?

In the Annex, you will find a pre-marital disclosure checklist, titled "What I really want to know about the couple", that the couple may find helpful.[71]

---

[71] The questions are in no way exhaustive and may be used as a starting point to a hopefully fruitful discussion.

Be it with your fiancée, your boyfriend/girlfriend or your best friends , the checklist can be used as an amusing insight into the other's perceptions and expectations of married life. Tick off the questions you'd like answered, switch the phrasing accordingly and watch as the other replies.

To ease the awkwardness in finding out about your partner's medical history, the couple could perhaps consider undergoing a medical examination together before marriage. A health check could be less confrontational because it involves an exchange of information and the medical report acts as a go-between in conveying sensitive information. Also, a medical examination would be a good supplement to the exchange of questions between the couple, bringing to light other information such as venereal disease and providing a look for example into one's family's medical history of illness such as diabetes, cancer and/or depression.

Really, the question should then be whether it is preferred to have the disclosure done before the couple starts dating on a more serious level or just before they get married. With emotions invested heavily into a relationship ready for marriage, the couple's judgment may become clouded with love and affection for the other. Notwithstanding this, disclosure will aid the transition from single to married life, preparing the couple for unexpected habits and traits that may reveal themselves during marriage.

Of course, the lists and methods suggested in achieving pre-marital disclosure are in no way all-inclusive. It is hoped that the categories above may spark a meaningful discussion between the couple prior to the wedding.

Chapter Three

The Third Step: Getting Married

Marriage is not a noun; it's a verb. It isn't something you get; it's something you do.

— *Barbara De Angelis*

After you and your spouse-to-be have decided to tie the knot, both parties will have to deal with the technicalities of getting legally married. Being aware of the various formalities and procedures will help make planning the Big Day easier in many aspects.

A marriage solemnized in Singapore is void unless it has been validly solemnized.

Only marriages solemnized on the authority of a valid marriage licence issued by the Registrar of Marriages or a valid special marriage licence granted by the Minister for Social and Family Development shall be valid.[1]

A marriage, whether solemnized in Singapore or elsewhere shall be void on certain grounds, including where:

1. At the date of the marriage, either of the parties is already married to another person; or[2]
2. Both parties are of the same sex.[3]

---

[1] Women's Charter (Cap 353, 2009 Rev Ed) s 22(1).
[2] *Id*, at s 11.
[3] *Id*, at s 12(1).

This chapter takes you through the procedure that must be followed in order to be legally married in Singapore.

OBTAINING A MARRIAGE LICENCE

Prior to solemnization conducted by the Registrar of Marriages or a licenced solemniser, a marriage licence must be obtained. A marriage licence, as its name suggests, permits the marriage to take place. This is not to be confused with a marriage certificate. A marriage certificate is legal proof of the legally valid union between the husband and wife.

An extra step applies for foreigners employed in Singapore on a work permit. They must obtain approval from the Ministry of Manpower prior to marrying a Singapore citizen or Permanent Resident and approval must be granted before the filing of notice of intended marriage.

Filing of Notice

The first action that you and your spouse-to-be need to undertake can be done right from the comfort of your homes. Both of you have to give notice to the Registrar of your intention to get married in the prescribed form.[4] This has to be electronically filed and submitted via the website of the Registry of Marriages. No other mode of application to file notices of intended marriage will be entertained.

Such a form requires the couple to provide their names, the names of their two elected witnesses and the date on which they would like to have the solemnization of their marriage conducted. It also allows the couple to decide there and then whether they prefer to have their wedding at the Registry of Marriages premises or any other venue chosen by the couple.

Payment of the prescribed fee can be done over the Internet as well. Upon payment, couples will be able to print out a statement, along with a set of instructions provided by the Registry of Marriages. This statement will include details of the solemnization, as well as declarations that they meet the statutory requirements to marry, amongst other things.

---

[4]*Id*, at s 14.

The notice filed will be put on public display and details of the notice will remain open for public search on the Registry of Marriages' website.[5] It is placed on public record so that anyone may file objections, if any.[6] This procedure is elaborated on further in our discussion below on 'filing of caveats'.

Document Verification & Statutory Declaration

In order to obtain a marriage licence, you and your spouse-to-be will need to attest to the details given and declare that both of you have fulfilled all the statutory requirements needed to enter into a legally valid marriage.[7] The couple typically makes a trip down to the Registry of Marriages before the solemnization to complete the paperwork.

The filing of notice as described in the earlier section includes the declaration that both you and your spouse-to-be meet the conditions before a marriage licence is issued.

The declarations include a certificate of completion of a marriage preparation programme or a certificate of attendance certified by the programme organiser, if applicable.

The marriage preparation programme is only required if any of the marrying parties is a Singapore Citizen or a Permanent Resident; and

1. Where at least one party is aged below eighteen years old; or
2. Where both parties are aged eighteen years and above but below twenty-one years of age.

Additionally, divorcees are required to make a declaration of any existing maintenance debts owed to their ex-spouse or child. This is aimed at providing a full disclosure to future partners, as well as to remind the divorcee of his or her persisting familial commitments to his or her previous marriage.

Document verification is conducted to allow the relevant authorities to check the details so declared. Documents that need to be verified will be listed in the filing instructions given along with the printed statement of notice. Once

---

[5] *Id*, at s 16(2).
[6] *Id*, at s 19.
[7] *Id*, at s 17.

verified, the couple then makes a formal statutory declaration that involves them stating that all details given in the statutory declaration form are true.

The couple's statutory declarations have to be sworn or affirmed by each of the parties and made in the presence of each other before a Commissioner for Oaths. They will need to arrange for such a meeting by appointment.

The document verification process leading up to the statutory declaration made before the Commissioner for Oaths should not be taken lightly. A false declaration is an offence that may result in the offender being sent to prison for a term up to three years, in addition to a fine.[8]

Filing of Caveats

Any person with an objection to the marriage may file a caveat with the Registry of Marriages after the notice of intended marriage has been given. A caveat is basically an objection or a notice of "alert" brought against the issuance of a marriage licence. The person with the objection will need to provide supporting documents to evidence his or her reason for objecting. An example would be a concerned aunt objecting to the marriage because she has proof that the spouse-to-be is still undergoing divorce proceedings that has yet to be finalised.

The filing of a caveat is not uncommon or difficult to do in practice. When an objection has been filed, the Registrar will not issue a licence unless the caveat is withdrawn. The Registrar may still proceed with the issuance of a marriage licence if he thinks that the caveat filed is not sufficient to obstruct the grant of the licence. Ultimately, the Registrar retains the discretion to refer the matter to the High Court.[9]

Where no objections to the filed notice of marriage have been made or where a caveat has been withdrawn or the Registrar of Marriages deems the caveat should not obstruct the issue of a licence and where the required document verification and statutory declarations have been carried out and completed, the Registrar shall, after the expiration of 21 days from the date of the notice of the intended marriage, issue a marriage licence that is valid for 3 months from the date of the said notice. If the marriage does not take place within 3 months after the date of the said notice, the said notice and all

---

[8]Oaths and Declarations Act (Cap. 211, 2001 Rev Ed) s 14.
[9]*Supra* n 1, at ss 20(1) & (2).

consequent proceedings shall be void and fresh notice must be given before the parties can lawfully marry.[10]

Special Instances

Unlike the typical marriage licence that is granted by the Registrar, a special marriage licence is granted by the Minister for Social and Family Development. This licence may be issued when either of the parties is below the age of 18 years old.[11] A special marriage licence is valid only for one month from the date of issue.

Separately, a licence may be granted by the Minister to parties who fall within what is described in the Women's Charter as "prohibited degrees of relationship" (e.g. where a man intends to marry his mother's sister), if the Minister is satisfied that the marriage is valid under "the law, religion, custom or usage which would have been applicable to the parties thereto if this Act had not been enacted".[12] This step taken by the Minister would have to be based on an inquiry into the facts of the particular case.

SOLEMNIZATION

Once you and your spouse-to-be have obtained a licence to marry, you can proceed onto the next step to being recognised as having a legally valid marriage.

Details of solemnization would have been decided when both of you filed your notice of marriage. Thus, you and your spouse-to-be will have to comply with the choices that both of you made earlier on. For example, only certain dates can be chosen for solemnization after the notice of marriage is filed. Also, in the case of a marriage licence, the date chosen must be within a period after the expiry of 21 days but before the expiry of 3 months, starting from the date of notice filed and upon payment of the prescribed fees.[13]

---

[10]*Id*, at s 18.
[11]*Id*, at s 21.
[12]*Id*, at s 10.
[13]*Id*, at s 17(1).

The two witnesses named in the notice filed must also be present at the solemnization.[14] These two witnesses, along with both you and your spouse-to-be and the licenced solemnizer, will need to sign on the marriage certificate at the solemnization ceremony, after the exchange of your marriage vows.

Licenced solemnizers are persons appointed by the Minister for Social and Family Development. You will need to contact a licenced solemnizer preferably 3 to 4 months before the solemnization. This would mean contact with the licensed solemnizer should be made even in advance of the filing of notice. Once contacted, a licensed solemnizer can choose to accept or reject the invitation to officiate at the wedding. The licensed solemnizer accepts by signing a Solemnizer Consent Form.[15]

A valid solemnization requires various conditions to be fulfilled. However, the particular form and ceremony that is to be conducted such as the venue and vows exchanged, is not critical to its validity. The Women's Charter leaves it to the Registrar or the licenced solemnizer to solemnize the marriage in whatever form and ceremony as the Registrar or the licensed solemnizer deems fit, so long as the ceremony is done in accordance with the law, religion, custom or usage of the parties or any of the parties thereto.[16]

However, it remains unchanged that during the solemnization, the Registrar or licenced solemnizer will have to request each of the parties to the marriage to declare that he or she is willing to take the other party as his or her wedded wife or husband.[17] This would normally be constituted in a romantic exchange of marriage vows, and the heart-thumping finale of the "I do"s.

Proper Solemnization of your Marriage

It is important for you and your spouse-to-be to follow proper procedures in solemnizing your marriage. Failure intentionally to observe the proper procedures, such as going through the solemnization process without receipt of a marriage licence, or after the expiration of three months from the date of the notice of the intended marriage or in the absence of two credible

---

[14]*Id*, at s 22(2).

[15]The form is available for download on the Registry of Marriages' website.

[16]*Supra* n 1, at s 23 read with s 2.

[17]*Id*, at s 23.

witnesses, are offences and could result in punishments being meted out against you and your spouse-to-be if found guilty.[18]

REGISTRATION OF SOLEMNIZATION

Marriages solemnized by the Registrar are immediately registered and the certificate of marriage issued, a sealed copy of which is delivered to the couple.[19] For marriages not solemnized by the Registrar, registration is to be done within a month of the marriage. This is done by:

1. Producing either oral or documentary evidence of the marriage before the Deputy Registrar as he or she may require;
2. Furnishing such particulars as may be required by the Deputy Registrar for the due registration of the marriage; and
3. As for foreign marriages, the Registrar has the power to register foreign marriages that have been solemnized outside Singapore but are not yet registered in Singapore.[20]

There is no provision in the Women's Charter that empowers the Registrar to re-register foreign marriages. The power of the Registrar to register foreign marriages only extends to those that are yet to be registered in Singapore.

If you and your spouse had your marriage solemnized outside Singapore, both of you can apply for voluntary registration of your marriage.[21] In such cases, the Registrar will only refuse to enter the marriage into the Register if he is satisfied that your marriage is void under the provisions of the Women's Charter.[22]

While the law does not require foreign marriages to be registered locally and generally accepts foreign marriage certificates as evidence of marriage,[23] registering your foreign marriage may be useful for various reasons. This would give the assurance and convenience a Singapore marriage certificate issued in consequence of the act of registration can bring

---

[18]*Id*, at s 40.
[19]*Id*, at s 28(1).
[20]*Id*, at s 29(1).
[21]*Id*, at s 182(1).
[22]*Id*, at s 182(5).
[23]Registry of Marriage website — FAQ — Preparation for Marriage.

for the purposes of HDB flat purchase applications.[24] The original certificate of marriage should be kept safely as some Singapore authorities such as the Central Provident Fund Board would need the production of the original or certified true copy of the Marriage Certificate as proof.

MARRIAGE CEREMONIES

Both you and your spouse-to-be may choose to add a customary and/or religious marriage ceremony to the solemnization of your marriage which may be conducted before, after or even in conjunction with the solemnization itself. The customary and/or religious marriage ceremony however, is not the solemnization of the marriage itself.

A customary and/or religious marriage ceremony is not mandatory but may be required by the custom or religion of either or both of the parties. There is no set ordering of ceremonies either. Yet, having a Chinese tea ceremony for example is a time-honoured ritual that many Chinese couples choose to follow. Couples are also able to exchange their marriage vows again at their customary and/or religious marriage ceremony if they so wish.

Increasingly, couples prefer to combine the solemnization and the customary and/or religious marriage ceremony, as they feel it marks the commencement of their married life together and makes the event more meaningful.

---

[24]*Local Developments on Foreign Marriages and Divorce,* Singapore Academy of Law Journal (1994) Vol 6 at p 461.

Chapter Four

The Fourth Step: Happily Married

You don't marry one person; you marry three: the person you think they are, the person they are, and the person they are going to become as a result of being married to you.

— *Richard Needham*

After the vows are exchanged and the Rubicon crossed, the couple may feel a range of unexpected emotions. The couple may realise that their expectations of marriage were unrealistic. Or they may be spurred into a state of bliss more intense than when they were honeymooning. These emotions can be so varied because marriage affects each and everyone differently, and affects all aspects of life – not just the romantic and emotional but also the legal, financial, social, psychological and spiritual.

It is important to know how being married influences the legal status of each spouse. This chapter will discuss some of the legal rights and obligations of both spouses, the capacity of married women, and the financial obligations which arise in a marital relationship.

LEGAL RIGHTS

Sustaining a lasting and happy marital relationship is the most challenging aspect of marriage. Each party may have to make fundamental changes and compromises to his or her habits to adapt to the daily routine of the significant other. Such changes are sometimes essential to the upkeep of the spousal relationship. Yet, there is little the law can do to regulate married life as it remains an undeniably private affair.

The law chooses not to interfere unless necessary. Accordingly, you will see that the legal rights of a person do not change radically if you were to compare his or her rights before and after marriage. Instead, the law lists general reminders of what married life is believed to entail. Couples are encouraged to co-operate with each other in the interests of their marriage and where it applies, for the sake of their children. The married couple is also reminded that they are partners with equal decision-making power, in matrimony and for life.

Women's Charter (Cap. 353)

Rights and duties

46. — (1) Upon the solemnization of marriage, the husband and the wife shall be mutually bound to co-operate with each other in safeguarding the interests of the union and in caring and providing for the children.

...

46. — (4) The husband and the wife shall have equal rights in the running of the matrimonial household.

The relationship between the couple is that of equal co-operative partners. In line with this philosophy, married couples are encouraged to make decisions together. The views and opinions of one party are placed on par with the other, encouraging the precepts of respect and consensual decision-making.

The concept of mutual co-operation in marriage explains why, in any dissolution of marriage, matrimonial assets[1] are generally deemed to belong to both the husband and wife regardless of who had paid for them. It

---

[1] Women's Charter (Cap. 353, 2009 Rev Ed) s 112(10).

additionally alludes to why a child is the shared responsibility of his or her parents, regardless of the parent's gender or state of employment.

Existing Individual Rights Continues Into Marriage

As mentioned previously, marriage does not radically alter the legal rights enjoyed separately by the couple before marriage.

Women's Charter (Cap. 353)

Rights and duties

46. — (2) The husband and the wife shall have the right separately to engage in any trade or profession or in social activities.

46. — (3) The wife shall have the right to use her own surname and name separately.

Setting out the rights and duties of husband and wife is especially important where individuals fear a loss of their individual identity after marriage because their married lives are so intertwined with the other. To emphasise the individual rights a married person has, the law recognises the two spouses as two distinct legal entities.

Freedom of Trade or Profession

The husband and the wife each has equal and separate rights to engage in any trade, profession or social activity he or she chooses. This right subtly protects a spouse from being forced to leave his or her profession against his or her wishes. Following from this, whether the wife becomes a homemaker or continues to work is a decision that may be made by the wife independently. The converse is also true — a wife does not have the right to stop or force her husband to remain in work after marriage unless he wishes to.

Nonetheless, because marriage is a cooperative venture, both the husband and wife ought to be comfortable with the proposed employment arrangements of the other. The final decision ought to be made on a mutually satisfactory basis to satisfy and upkeep the happy union.

Right to Use Surname

Each individual has a right to change his or her name, as long as the proper procedure is followed. That is why the wife has several options with regard to her surname post-marriage. A married woman can choose to:

- adopt her husband's surname; or
- retain her maiden name;[2] or
- add her husband's surname to hers to form a hyphenated surname.

Should the wife elect to change her surname and/or her name, the procedure to be followed is relatively straightforward.

1. The wife must first execute a deed poll. This is a legal document dealing with a legal change of surname or name.
2. The wife must then approach the Immigration and Checkpoints Authority to apply for a change to her name in her identity card and passport. A separate application is required for a fresh passport to be issued in the new name.[3] A deed poll is useful to provide evidence of change of name especially if the wife is holding assets in her maiden name so that there is no confusion later should she sell her assets.

   Alternatively, a wife can simply add her married name to her identity card. This can be done without a deed poll. Again, a separate application for a fresh passport with her new name is required.[4]

   Some women may not wish to have their names changed, especially if they have only chosen to get married later in their lives and have already established themselves in their field of work with their maiden name. Some may even see the act of changing their surname as relinquishing their own identity. The law has adopted a flexible approach, allowing the wife options in this aspect of married life.

---

[2]*Id*, at s 46(3).

[3]More information can be found on the website of the Immigration and Checkpoints Authority (ICA) at <http://www.ica.gov.sg/page.aspx?pageid=140>.

[4]*Ibid*.

Reconciling Individual Rights and Joint Decisions

It is confusing that the law chooses to recognise individual rights, as well as incorporate principles of mutuality and partnership within the institution of marriage. The two seem to conflict and are indeed difficult to reconcile.

For instance, spouses may not have the luxury of exercising their right to remain unemployed if their family unit is in need of a stable income. A husband may choose to stay unemployed, but if that choice does not have his wife's support and is detrimental to the family unit as a whole, that exercise of independence may cost him his marriage and maybe even his case in family court.

Family decisions should be based on mutual agreement and both spouses must be comfortable with the arrangement proposed, be it the method of bringing up their child or the family's source of financial support.

The law chooses not to interfere with a decision made by the married couple unless intervention is necessary. The law takes on a more active role during divorce proceedings as this is when the two parties are more likely to be acrimonious and unlikely to be able to come to a fair conclusion or decision on their own. Till then, the Women's Charter assumes that spouses exercise their rights in a reasonable fashion, in light of the financial and other needs of their family unit.

Conjugal Rights and Privileges

Once a legally valid marriage is solemnized, the newlyweds enjoy certain conjugal rights. These are generally the rights and privileges that arise from a person's married status and include mutual rights of companionship, aid, and ongoing and exclusive sexual relations between spouses.

Running of the Matrimonial Household

The husband and the wife have equal rights to the running of the matrimonial household. This encompasses many decisions, including for example, whether a domestic helper should be hired and whether a joint bank account should be maintained.

The presence of equal rights in this area of law suggests that marriage is an equal and co-operative partnership. The partnership does not only recognise monetary contribution, but non-monetary contribution to the matrimonial relationship as well. As a result, where one party is the sole breadwinner of the family while the other takes care of housekeeping matters, such arrangements are treated as collaborative pursuits by both husband and wife and made in the interests of the marriage.

Exclusivity of Sexual Relations

The courts recognise that sexual relations are important in a healthy marriage and the law grants that exclusively to the husband and wife. Following from the point that a marriage provides a right to healthy sexual relations, a marriage may be voidable if it has not been consummated. That is to say, if a marriage is not consummated due to one spouse's inability or wilful refusal to do so, the other will have an option to have the marriage made void by obtaining an annulment.[5]

Celibacy Within Marriage[6]

A newly married couple remained sexually inactive even though the wife requested and placed herself in situations that normally would have led to sexual intercourse. The wife was attractive and was confused as to why her husband kept refusing her advances. In fact, she made at least six good attempts to seduce him but the husband refused to consummate the marriage. He remained faithful but refused to have sexual intercourse with her. After two years, the wife decided she had enough and brought her husband to court.

The judge concluded that the 29-year old should not be expected or made to wait any longer to consummate the marriage. Hence, the marriage was declared void.

---

[5]*Supra* n 1, at ss 106(a)–(b).
[6]*Tan Lan Eng v Lim Swee Eng* [1993] 3 SLR(R) 347; [1993] SGHC 258.

In most cases, marriage involves an ongoing sexual relationship between spouses. The law seems to reflect this stance that the right to sexual relations extends to continued consummation. What would the legal position be if the wife refuses to engage in sexual relations after the initial consummation of marriage?

The Penal Code provides that non-consensual penetration by a man of his wife's vagina using his penis, will not constitute the offence of "rape" except in limited circumstances.[7] Effectively, a husband who forces his unwilling wife to have sexual intercourse with him will be exempt from the charge of rape. This is known as the marital rape exception.

Did you know?

Penetration of body orifices other than the vagina does not constitute rape. If a man penetrates a woman's mouth or anus with his penis without her consent, he commits an offence known as sexual assault by penetration but not rape.[8] This is because rape is defined as a man's penis penetrating the woman's vagina without consent.[9]

However, the wife is not without any legal recourse if she gets physically hurt or restrained. If the elements of the relevant offence are proven, the law provides that the husband may be found guilty of voluntarily causing hurt,[10] voluntarily causing grievous hurt,[11] or wrongful restraint,[12] all of which are offences under Singapore criminal law. Also, if a husband resorts to violence and forces himself on his wife, or continually harasses her to cause anguish, it can amount to "family violence".[13] The wife may in response take out a Personal Protection Order against the husband. With the Personal Protection

---

[7] Penal Code (Cap. 224, 2008 Rev Ed) s 375(4).
[8] *Id*, at s 376(1).
[9] *Id*, at s 375(1).
[10] *Id*, at s 321.
[11] *Id*, at s 322.
[12] *Id*, at s 339.
[13] For the definition of family violence, see *supra* n 1, at s 64.

Order, the marital rape exception will not apply.[14] The legal recourse to a Personal Protection Order is also available to any family member affected by family violence.[15]

Further, if his wife is living apart from him under an interim judgment of divorce or a written separation agreement or due to the commencement of divorce proceedings, a husband who has sexual intercourse with her and without her consent commits the offence of rape.[16]

A wife's mere intention to separate from her husband is not enough for her to argue that sexual intercourse without her consent constitutes rape. Only where formal legal steps have been taken towards separation or divorce, or where the woman has obtained specific court orders such as a Personal Protection Order can the husband be charged with rape. Otherwise, he can avail himself of the marital rape exception.

Marital Rape in the News

In recent times, there has been public discourse on the controversial topic of marital rape. "No to Rape" for example, is a local volunteer project that advocates against all forms of sexual violence, including marital rape. In 2010, a petition was prepared for the attention of our Prime Minister and signed by over 3600 signatories.[17]

Repealing the marital rape exception will bring Singapore in line with jurisdictions such as the United Kingdom and the United States of America.

The Women's Charter strives to adopt a reasonable approach to matters relating to marriage, including that of sexual expectations. One possible reason for the existence of the marital rape exception in Singapore is that the law on this issue relies mainly on the good sense of a spouse not to resort to sexual violence and intimidation. The law also relies on the goodwill and love the couple has for each other to refrain from hurting each other. Ultimately, a healthy sexual relationship is a special bond that spouses share

---

[14]*Supra* n 7, at s 375(4)(d).

[15]*Supra* n 1, at s 65(1).

[16]*Supra* n 7, at s 375(4)(a).

[17]More information on the organisation can be found on <www.notorape.com/petition/>.

within the confines of their loving marriage and accordingly, the law chooses to leave the couple to their own choices.

Privileged Communication

Communication is undeniably one of the key tenets of a sustainable marriage and secrets between husband and wife are usually kept to a minimum. The law reflects that position by providing that marital communications are privileged and by preventing disclosure of such privileged communication in court save in exceptional circumstances.

Evidence Act (Cap. 97)

Communications during marriage

124 — No person who is or has been married shall be compelled to disclose any communication made to him during marriage by any person to whom he is or has been married; nor shall he be permitted to disclose any such communication unless the person who made it or his representative in interest consents, except in suits between married persons or proceedings in which one married person is prosecuted for any crime committed against the other.

Where the husband and wife confide in each other during the marriage, the spouse to whom the matters are communicated cannot be forced to disclose those matters; even if he or she was willing to disclose them, he or she cannot do so without the other's consent. Disclosure of privileged communication during marriage is permitted in proceedings between the married couple themselves and proceedings in which a spouse or former spouse is prosecuted for any crime committed by that spouse against the other spouse or former spouse.

Confessions of a Murderer[18]

L was arrested for the murder of a childhood friend. On the day of the murder, L's wife recalled seeing blood on his toes. L later confessed to his

---

[18]*Lim Lye Hock v Public Prosecutor* [1995] 1 SLR 238; [1994] SGCA 121.

wife that he killed the deceased by hitting her with a stick and then a big stone.

At trial, the court found that L's confession to his wife was "marital communication" and that she could not be forced to disclose what he told her. Furthermore, even if she was prepared to disclose the communication, she was not permitted to do so without L's consent. However, she was allowed to tell the court of the fact that she saw blood on his toes, as this was an observation by her rather than something L had expressly told her.

Conferring such a privilege may prove to be frustrating in court particularly where there is only one witness qualified to testify, and that witness is a spouse who could potentially be exempted from testifying. Yet, the law is swayed towards upholding familial values in this aspect, choosing to respect the couple's privacy and personal choices so as to not deter spousal communication and ultimately, to safeguard harmony within the family unit.

CAPACITY OF MARRIED WOMEN

In traditional Asian society, the husband is more often than not regarded as the head of the family while the wife takes care of the domestic chores and the upbringing of the children, sometimes above and beyond a daytime job.[19]

Against this backdrop, the Women's Charter, when it was originally enacted in 1961, was designed amongst other things, to protect women in Singapore and to clarify the laws covering the rights and duties of married persons, the maintenance of wives and children, and the punishment of crimes against women and girls. As a result, the legal provisions we read today may appear to favour women. These provisions (like the one set out below) should not be viewed as biased in favour of women, but rather as necessary to clarify and balance the positions of husband and wife in

---

[19]For reference, please see our earlier discussion about women being like chattels to their husbands in Chapter Two.

society.[20] They also help one to understand what to expect when he or she gets married.[21]

Women's Charter (Cap. 353)

Capacity of married women

51. — Subject to the provisions of this Act, a married woman shall —

(a) be capable of acquiring, holding and disposing of, any property;

(b) be capable of rendering herself, and being rendered, liable in respect of any tort, contract, debt or obligation;

(c) be capable of suing and being sued in her own name either in tort or in contract or otherwise and shall be entitled to all remedies and redress for all purposes; and

(d) be subject to the law relating to bankruptcy and to the enforcement of judgments and orders,

in all respects as if she were a feme sole.

PROPERTY RIGHTS

Property held or purchased by spouses during their marriage is not governed by Family Law but by the Law of Property. In some sense, the law sees the holding of assets between spouses as assets held by distinct strangers. An exception to this general rule is the concept of "matrimonial home" which will be discussed later.

Holding of Property during Marriage

The concept that individuals own their property in their own right is known as the doctrine of separation of property. This doctrine is applied in Singapore

---

[20] Compare these rights under S 51 of the Women's Charter to the rights of women in the 18th century before the feminist movement began.

[21] For more information about the relevance of the Women's Charter to modern-day Singapore, see the closing speech by Dr Vivian Balakrishnan in the Second Reading of the Women's Charter (Amendment) Bill on 10 January 2011 at <www.parliament.gov.sg>.

and consequently, the status of being married has no effect on the capacity of the husband and the wife to hold and transact property separately. Neither does a spouse obtain proprietary interests in the individual assets of the other spouse merely by marriage. Generally, the concept provides that the spouse who earns, buys or inherits the asset owns that asset. However in the event of a divorce and consequent partition of property, exceptions are allowed: where one spouse did not have a job but concentrated on keeping house and raising a family, the courts have ruled that that spouse is also entitled to a share of the matrimonial assets acquired or improved on during the marriage even when such assets may be in the sole name of the other spouse.

Purchase of Property

It is common for a married couple to own their place of residence. The couple may also choose to purchase other properties for investment and/or holiday purposes.

Such property can be held in sole names separately or in the joint names of both spouses. Where the property is held by the couple jointly, the law considers husband and wife to be co-owners. There are two types of ownership i.e. joint tenancy and tenancy-in-common. The biggest difference is the right of survivorship, which only applies to a joint tenancy.

Joint Tenancy and Tenancy-in-Common in a Nutshell[22]

A joint tenancy is a type of ownership where all co-owners have an equal undivided interest in the whole of the property regardless of each co-owner's financial contribution to the purchase. In fact, the default position is that if two or more persons acquire real property without specifying the manner of ownership, they will hold the property as joint tenants.[23] Upon the death of a joint tenant, his or her interest will automatically pass to the remaining registered joint tenant. This occurs regardless of whether the

---

[22]More information can be found on the Housing Development Board website <www.hdb.gov.sg>.
[23]Land Titles Act (Cap. 157, 2004 Rev Ed) s 53(1).

deceased joint tenant has left behind a Will giving away his or her share of the property to someone else. This concept is known as the right of survivorship.

In certain circumstances, the law will look beyond the joint tenancy and intervene to impose a tenancy-in-common.[24] It may also be that the intention of the joint tenants is for the right of survivorship to apply only upon the death of one of them, and for them to have completely different intentions to that of a joint tenancy while they are still alive.[25]

A tenancy-in-common on the other hand, is a form of ownership which enables each co-owner to hold a separate share in the property. All the co-owners are entitled to enjoy the whole property regardless of his or her share in the property. In a tenancy-in-common, the deceased's interest in the property does not pass automatically to the remaining co-owner(s) but goes to his or her estate. When a tenant-in-common dies, the deceased's interest passes to his beneficiary in accordance with his or her Will if there is one. Otherwise, the intestacy law of Singapore will apply.

FINANCIAL OBLIGATIONS

Never marry for money. Ye'll borrow it cheaper.

— Scottish proverb

Financial stress and money squabbles are often the focal point of a divorce. Therefore, it is important to ensure that each spouse is aware of and understands his or her respective financial obligations within the family unit.

---

[24]*Lau Siew Kim v. Teo Guan Chye Terence* [2008] 2 SLR(2) 108.

[25]In *Neo Hui Ling v. Ang Ah Sew* [2012] 2 SLR 831, the court found that while the daughter added her mother as a joint tenant of the property to provide her with a roof over her head upon the daughter's death, the daughter did not intend for the mother to have a share in the property while the daughter was alive.

Maintenance of Spouse

For more traditional couples, the husband may want to be the sole bread-winner and provide for his wife. Nowadays it is common for both spouses to work. The Women's Charter states unequivocally that the husband has a duty to provide reasonable maintenance for his wife during the marriage.[26] If a husband neglects or refuses to do so, a wife may apply to court for an order of maintenance to be granted.

These applications should be distinguished from the other category of maintenance application which arises only after a divorce has been granted. Here, we are referring to application made when a marriage is valid and subsisting at the time of application. The wife will need to convince the court that the grant of a maintenance order is reasonable on the facts and circumstances of her particular case, especially if she is working and can maintain herself.

The court will take into consideration all facts and circumstances. In reaching a decision on the issue of maintenance of the wife during the subsistence of the marriage, the court will consider, amongst others, the following factors:[27]

- Financial needs of the wife;
- Earning capacity of the wife and her other financial resources;
- Physical or mental disability of the wife;
- Standard of living enjoyed by the family before the refusal or neglect by husband; and
- The conduct of each party to the marriage.

This list is not exhaustive. The court sees all factors as relevant, including the gross misconduct of both parties. An example of gross misconduct is the acquisition or squandering of the other spouse's resources.[28] If a maintenance order is thought to be necessary, the order given may be in the form of a monthly allowance or a lump sum.

---

[26]*Supra* n 1, at s 69(1).

[27]*Supra* n 1, at s 69(4).

[28]Leong Wai Kum, Elements of Family Law in Singapore (LexisNexis, 2012) at p 459.

There is no corresponding duty on the part of a wife to maintain her husband; however, with the Women's Charter (Amendment) Bill 2016, incapacitated husbands and ex-husbands will be allowed to apply for spousal maintenance where there is a clear need.[29]

Maintenance of Children

Every parent has a legal duty to provide for his or her child. The law treats this duty with utmost seriousness and any court dealing with a child takes the welfare of the child as its most important consideration in coming to a decision. Naturally, a parent's duty will encompass a financial obligation to maintain the child and this duty must be carried out regardless of the state of marriage.

While all children are entitled to be nurtured to adulthood, there is no legal duty to maintain a child to an extravagent standard beyond the capabilities or means of the parents. Rather, the law seeks to ensure that the child receives an adequate level of maintenance which the parents are physically, emotionally and financially able to provide. This legal obligation to maintain a child continues till the child proceeds into adulthood at the age of 21. However, even if the child is beyond the age of 21, a child maintenance order may still be made if the child falls within one of the circumstances under section 69(5) of the Women's Charter.[30]

Women's Charter (Cap. 353)

69 — (2) A District Court or a Magistrate's Court may, on due proof that a parent has neglected or refused to provide reasonable maintenance for his child who is unable to maintain himself, order that parent to pay a monthly allowance or a lump sum for the maintenance of that child.

69 — (5) The court shall not make an order under subsection (2) for the benefit of a child who has attained the age of 21 years or for a period that extends beyond the day on which the child will attain that age unless

---

[29]See Women's Charter (Amendment) Bill 2016 s 69 and s 113.
[30]*Supra* n 1, at s 69(5).

the court is satisfied that the provision of the maintenance is necessary
because —

(a) of a mental or physical disability of the child;
(b) the child is or will be serving full-time national service;
(c) the child is or will be or (if an order were made under subsection
    (2)) would be receiving instruction at an educational establishment or
    undergoing training for a trade, profession or vocation, whether or
    not while in gainful employment, or
(d) special circumstances, other than those stated in paragraphs (a), (b)
    and (c), exist which justify the making of the order

Singapore has shown support for the rights of children by providing public
assistance for families in need, particularly in the areas of health care and
compulsory primary school education.[31] It has also affirmed internationally
the position of children by signing the United Nations Convention on Rights
of the Child.[32]

Maintenance of Aged Parents

Couples looking to get married may be faced with the dilemma of having to
take care of their parents and future parents-in-law. With multigenerational
households being the norm in Singapore, the financial cost of filial piety is
pertinent for couples.

In Singapore, aged parents who are unable to sufficiently support
themselves financially may apply to the Tribunal for the Maintenance of
Parents (and not the courts) for a Maintenance Order against their children
who are not supporting them financially.

To file an application for maintenance with the Tribunal, the parent must
be domiciled or resident in Singapore, be at least be 60 years old and be

---

[31] The example of primary school education is evidence by the Compulsory Education Act
(Cap 51, 2001 Rev Ed).
[32] United Nations Convention on the Rights of the Child 1989.

unable to support himself or herself adequately.[33] This is where the parent is unable to afford basic needs such as shelter, food and clothing. To evaluate this, the Tribunal will consider the parent's total or expected income and other financial resources available to him or her.

Exceptionally, a parent below 60 years old may file an application to apply for maintenance if he or she is unable to maintain himself or herself due to a physical or mental infirmity or if there is any other special reason.[34]

Not all eligible applicants head to a Tribunal hearing. Once an aged parent is assessed as eligible and it is decided that the claim of the aged parent should continue, conciliation officers at the Ministry of Social and Family Development are assigned to take on the role of mediating between the parties. Only when mediation fails is the case heard at the Tribunal.

Factors Considered at Tribunal Hearing

Even if the eligibility requirement is satisfied, the Tribunal will take further factors into account in determining whether the adult child must pay maintenance to his or her parent. One factor is the history relating to the parent's discharge of parental responsibility to the adult child. For example, the Tribunal might consider the children's reluctance to support a parent whose mistreatment of their mother left a lasting impression on them, and left them feeling bitter towards that parent.[35] Another factor the Tribunal considers is the adult child's own ability to support himself, his spouse and his children, which take precedence over the maintenance of parents.[36]

Ultimately, the Tribunal does not wish to enforce the concept of filial piety blindly. Filial piety is seen as a social responsibility rather than a legal requirement and there must be something more than a moral obligation for the Tribunal to invoke its powers to order maintenance.

---

[33]Maintenance of Parents Act (Cap 167B, 1996 Rev Ed) s 3(1).

[34]*Id*, at s 3(5).

[35]*LBH v LSK & Others* [2002] SGTMP 1.

[36]*Supra* n 35, at s 5(1)(a).

Poor Rich Dad[37]

A son brought an application for contributions to be made by his other siblings towards the monthly maintenance of their father who lived with the son's family. Their father had a stroke and required a live-in maid amongst other things.

It was revealed during the case that the father was rather wealthy and had RM 300,000 worth of interest-bearing bonds as well as an undivided half share in a basket of currencies worth $100,000 and was able to maintain himself adequately.

Taking these factors into account, the Tribunal decided that although the other siblings were not fulfilling their moral duty to take care of their father, this duty was in no way a legal one. Hence, the Tribunal was not in a position to enforce it.

Therefore, should there be unhappiness with the current financial or care arrangement adopted by the adult child or between a set of adult siblings, the proper setting for such dispute resolution may well be in mediation or family counselling. The Tribunal is not the proper forum for the resolution of any serious allegations. An open discussion may be sufficient to iron out any misunderstanding or to lead to a satisfactory outcome for both the child and the parent.

---

[37] LYS v LKH and Others [2002] SGTMP 2.

Chapter Five
The Baby Steps: Parenthood

Bring love into your home for this is where our love for each other must start.

— Mother Teresa

Some couples see having children as a tangible expression of the love between them. Other couples see it as a milestone, or as a post-marriage step sometimes taken at the urging of their parents, parents-in-law or their spouse. But where exactly does the law stand on this matter? What options are there with regard to family planning? This chapter seeks to discuss the topic of creating, maintaining and developing the family unit.

The More the Merrier
Jim Bob Duggar was born on 18 July, 1965 in Arkansas, United States of America. He was a real estate agent, and a former state legislator who served in the Arkansas House of Representatives from 1999 to 2002. Jim Bob married his wife Michelle Ruark in 1984. The Duggars see children as a blessing,[1] and over the course of their marriage, Jim Bob and Michelle raised 19 children: Joshua, Jana, John-David, Jill, Jessa, Jinger, Joseph, Josiah, Joy-Anna, Jedidiah, Jeremiah, Jason, James, Justin, Jackson, Johannah, Jennifer, Jordyn-Grace and Josie.

---

[1] More information on the family can be found on <www.duggarfamily.com>.

Absence of Obligation to Bear Children

Whether or not the husband and wife want to have a child is a decision for both of them to make together. Hence courts generally do not interfere with autonomous decisions made by the husband and wife relating to childbearing and the use of contraceptives.[2] However, conflicts concerning issues of childbearing and the use of contraceptives or termination of pregnancy may still amount to unreasonable behaviour, such that the conflict may legitimately qualify as a fact that supports the ground for divorce.

ABORTIONS

The public is at once pro-choice and pro-life.

— Karlyn Bowman

In Singapore, a woman has a legal right to an abortion if she so wishes, as long as she satisfies the conditions laid down in the Termination of Pregnancy Act. Under the Act, a husband's or boyfriend's consent is not a pre-requisite for having the abortion carried out and the woman need not legally seek the approval nor consider objections put forward by the husband or the boyfriend.

Following this, a husband or boyfriend can be convicted for compelling or inducing his wife or girlfriend to have an abortion, be it by coercion or intimidation. A fine of up to $3,000 or imprisonment for up to three years or both may be imposed if he is found guilty.[3]

An abortion must satisfy, inter alia, the statutory requirements stated below:

1. The pregnant woman requests for the abortion and consents to it in writing;
2. The pregnancy has progressed not more than 24 weeks; and
3. The abortion is carried out by an authorised medical practitioner in an approved institution.

---

[2] *Kwong Sin Hwa v Lau Lee Yen* [1993] SGCA 6 at [38].
[3] Termination of Preganancy Act (Cap. 324, 1985 Rev Ed) s 5.

In Singapore, the patient has to undergo compulsory counselling prior to the abortion. A mandatory 48-hour waiting period is also imposed before the abortion can be carried out. As a result, she is given more time to consider the possible implications of the procedure.[4]

Factors to Consider

While medical advancement has greatly reduced the risks of having an abortion, one should also consider other angles of this procedure.[5]

An abortion patient may have social, psychological, spiritual and cultural consequences to consider, as abortion affects the body, heart and mind, and some people believe, the soul us well.

Singapore is a multi-religious country with a diverse ethnic mix of people from different countries and different races. The main religions in Singapore include Buddhism, Christianity, Hinduism, Islam[6] and Taoism.[7] For many people, their views on abortion will be influenced by their religious or spiritual beliefs.

Ultimately the decision whether or not to have an abortion is personal to the pregnant woman and should be carefully made. In law, the expectant mother has the sole right to decide whether or not she wishes to give birth to the child.

At the same time, since a marriage is an equal co-operative partnership, the husband also ought to have his wishes respected and considered by his wife. The question of whether to have an abortion is a serious decision that should be made not just by the wife but jointly by the couple.

---

[4]More information on the abortion procedures and regulations involved can be found on <www.aware.org.sg/information/abortion/>.

[5]Interestingly, it was for this reason that a similar Act was passed in England. This subsequently led to the legalisation of abortion in England.

[6]As this book does not discuss Muslim marriages, the Muslim position on abortion will not be discussed.

[7]*Census of Population 2010 Statistical Release 1: Demographic Characteristics, Education, Language and Religion, Singapore Department of Statistics*, available at <www.singstat. gov.sg>.

ADOPTION

Adoption is not about finding children for families, it's about finding families for children.

— Joyce Maguire Pavao

Adoption is becoming an increasingly viable and common option for couples all over the world, including those in Singapore, for a variety of reasons. Infertile couples who wish to have a child may turn to adoption while others may feel a calling to help children. Whatever the reason, commercial agencies have quickly picked up on this increasing demand, complementing the existing governmental agencies that promote and support adoption and the family units involved. These agencies, both commercial and public, continue to support couples throughout the adoption process to make it easier for couples to follow the mandated adoption procedures. A child should not be adopted on a whim because it is a decision that will last a lifetime and unlike a purchased good from a store, a child cannot be returned.

In order to safeguard the interests of the child, the then Ministry of Community Development, Youth and Sports introduced a new initiative in 2012, making it compulsory for prospective adopters to attend a pre-adoption briefing prior to making an application to court for an Adoption Order. During the briefing, prospective adopters are educated, inter alia, on the adoption process, their potential rights and responsibilities as adoptive parents, and the general and special needs of an adopted child.

Only then may the couple make an application to the Family Court for an adoption order to adopt a local child. This adoption order gives the adoption legal recognition in Singapore.

The Adoption of Children Act governs the law in Singapore on adoption. The legislation aims to safeguard the interests of the child and ensure that the prospective adopters are of sufficient maturity. The following conditions must be fulfilled before an adoption order can be made:

1. The child that is to be adopted must be under 21;[8]

---

[8]Adoption of Children Act (Cap. 4, 2012 Rev Ed) s 3(2).

2. The potential adoptive parents are to be over 25;[9] and
3. An age difference of at least 21 years must exist between the adoptive parent and child.[10]

However, slight flexibility is given in determining the latter two requirements. They may be waived should the court think fit and an exception might be granted where the applicant and child are closely related by blood. One example is the adoption of a niece or nephew.[11]

Different rules apply for international or cross-country adoptions and inquiries can be made at the appropriate government or private organisations for further information.

SPERM, EGG AND EMBRYO DONATION

Society is no stranger to medical procedures such as in-vitro fertilisation, a medical procedure that has been available to couples with difficulties in conception for many years now. Recent medical advances have now made gamete and embryo donation available as alternatives for couples who yearn for a child and yet are unable to produce naturally.[12] New religious concerns have arisen as a result. For example, the Catholic Church is not in favour of the use of assisted reproduction techniques.[13]

The Science Simplified

The female gamete is the egg and the male gamete is the sperm. Donated gametes are extracted, frozen and kept for the purposes of fertilisation. Once the egg is fertilised with the sperm, it becomes an embryo. Generally

---

[9] *Id*, at s 4(1)(a).

[10] *Id*, at s 4(1)(b).

[11] *Id*, at s 4(2).

[12] For example, South-east Asia and Singapore's first sperm bank was set up in 1977.

[13] For more information, see *"The Religious Concerns with IVF"* by Chip Marsden, <http://people.opposingviews.com/religious-concerns-ivf-5044.html>.

around the end of eight weeks, the embryo develops into a fetus and eventually, if all goes well, a child will be born.

The harvesting and banking of sperm which survives the husband now enables the widow to have the option of impregnating herself after her husband's death. Preserving both spouses' gametes keeps the option of hiring a surrogate mother open even after menopause. Embryo donation on the other hand, is usually offered by couples who have successfully undergone the in-vitro fertilisation process and who are left with embryos that they no longer require.

Sperm banks and egg donation centers in Singapore are unable to meet demand as there are few donations. In fact, it has been reported that for every sperm donation in Singapore, there are about eight couples seeking donors.[14] Hence, couples often resort to getting their own donors through other means, including via online websites or by searching for them overseas.[15] Donor anonymity is not always kept when donors are sourced locally without the help of fertility clinics in Singapore. It is possible that the two parties meet for an exchange of particulars or just for a friendly chat. This raises the question of future parental responsibility as it is currently unclear whether the law will hold the donor responsible for the upbringing of the child or if the donor can claim parental rights over the child later on in the child's life.

Due to the moral and religious issues involved in using assisted reproduction techniques, a couple should read widely and do in-depth research and reflection before deciding to use these techniques to have a baby.

---

[14]*Managing legal uncertainty in sperm donation*, The Straits Times, Pg A33, 2 December 2010.

[15]*Report: Lack of donors leaves Singapore sperm banks dry amid baby crisis*, Associated Press Worldstream, 3 October 2004 available at <https://www.highbeam.com/doc/1P1-91974786.html>.

What a Mix-Up![16]

There was once a mix-up of sperm at a Singapore fertility centre. There were two semen specimens in the laboratory from two different donors. The wrong sperm was used to create a 'test-tube baby' for a Singaporean Chinese woman and her Caucasian spouse.

Although the couple decided to keep the child, this matter created a huge up-roar and probably caused worry for potential donors.

The centre was slapped with a $20,000 fine after pleading guilty to breaching a condition of its Ministry of Health licence and the Centre was suspended from engaging in assisted reproduction procedures.

Some of the uncertainties surrounding issues in relation to the legal status of children conceived through assisted reproductive procedures were resolved with the coming into operation of the Status of Children (Assisted Reproductive Technology) Act 2013 (Act 16 of 2013) on 1 October 2014 ("the Act").[17] The Act clarified the legal parentage and status of children conceived through the use of assisted reproductive procedures where the wrong egg, sperm or embryo was used in the fertilisation process, and modernises the laws relating to legitimacy and to evidence of paternity.

The Act also made consequential amendments to section 114 of the Evidence Act to allow for scientific evidence such as DNA tests to be adduced before the court to displace the presumption of paternity.[18] Previously, section 114 of the Evidence Act conclusively presumed the legitimacy of a child born during the marriage, unless the husband could prove that he had no access to the wife when the child was conceived. Further, the Act also amended the Legitimacy Act to allow for the legitimisation of an illegitimate child whose parents marry subsequently, where either the father or mother was or is domiciled in Singapore at the date of the marriage. Previously, the Legitimacy Act provided for the legitimisation of an illegitimate child

---

[16]The fertility centre in Singapore was fined $20,000.00 for semen mix-up, according to AsiaOne, 22 June 2011.

[17]Correct at time of writing (February 2014).

[18]Evidence Act (Cap. 97, 1997 Rev Ed) s 114.

whose parents marry subsequently only when the father of the child was or is domiciled in Singapore at the date of the marriage.[19]

The premise of the Act is that a child conceived through assisted reproductive procedures should have at least one legal parent and puts the welfare and best interests of such a child first. In unfortunate cases where a mix-up has occurred, the Act ensures that the child is not left parentless after the mix-up is discovered. The court is also given flexibility to declare parentage where a different result would be in the best interests of the child, and takes into account factors such as the child's wishes and the bond the child has developed with any party.

Couples whose children were conceived using such procedures or are considering using these procedures to have children may have worried about the legitimacy and status of their children, particularly in unfortunate cases where a mix-up occurred in the fertilisation process. The Act may go some way to alleviate some of the concerns of such couples. However, they should also note that the scope of the Act is limited (for example, it does not deal with surrogacy issues nor cover situations such as egg-freezing). Whether its application will be expanded in future to include situations currently excluded remains to be seen.

ILLEGITIMATE CHILDREN

There are no illegitimate children — only illegitimate parents

— Leon R. Yankwich

Where the matter concerns a child born out of wedlock, the law seeks to protect the child's rights. This protection is accomplished by expanding the legal definition of a "legitimate child". For instance, a child born to a married couple whose marriage subsequently becomes annulled is nevertheless deemed a legitimate child under the Women's Charter.[20] Further,

---

[19]Legitimacy Act (Cap. 162, 1985 Rev Ed) s 3(1).
[20]Women's Charter (Cap. 353, 2009 Rev Ed) s 111(1).

in a void marriage which both parties reasonably believed to be valid, the law recognises the child of such a marriage as legitimate, even though it does not recognise the marriage as having existed at all.[21] This widening of the class of legitimate children also had the ripple effect of equalising the rights and privileges given to both legitimate and illegitimate children.

However, there is still a residual effect stemming from a relationship between a parent and illegitimate child. The following are some examples:

- An illegitimate child born in Singapore will not acquire citizenship by birth if only the father is a Singapore citizen. However, citizenship may still be granted in such cases if an application is made and the government considers it just and fair to do so taking into consideration all the circumstances at the time of application.[22] The child will acquire Singapore citizenship by birth if the mother is a Singapore citizen.[23]

- Under the Adoption Act, an adoption order may be made authorising the adoption of an infant (i.e. a person under 21 years of age) by the mother or father of the infant, either alone or jointly with her or his spouse.[24] An adoption order will not be made without the consent of every person or body who is a parent or guardian of the child to be adopted.[25] Where the child is illegitimate, the "father" of such a child is defined to mean the natural father; the definition of the word "parent" (of such a child) does not include the natural father. This means that the mother of an illegitimate child has a prior right to adopt the child; the child may also be put up for adoption without the father's consent.

- If a child is illegitimate and the father is not an informant of the birth, the illegitimate child takes on the surname of the mother.[26] The child's surname may not be problematic where there is no acrimony between the unmarried couple but it may be an issue where the relationship between the couple has turned sour.

---

[21] *Id*, at s 111(2).

[22] Constitution of the Republic of Singapore (1999 Reprint) Article 121.

[23] *Id*, Third Schedule s 15(1).

[24] *Supra* n 9, at s 3(4).

[25] *Id*, at s 4(4).

[26] Registration of Births and Deaths Act (Cap. 267, 1985 Rev Ed) s 10(1).

Financial Implications

Two financial concerns are that of an illegitimate child's entitlement to assets and maintenance from a parent.

Succession and Intestate Succession

One key issue with having an illegitimate child is the inability of parents to divide their assets equally amongst children with different legal status in cases where both the parents pass away without leaving a Will (i.e. intestate). Under those circumstances, the law allows equal portions of the intestate estate to be distributed among all children of the deceased. Yet, the term "child" in the Intestate Succession Act (Cap. 146) excludes the class of illegitimate children, placing them at a disadvantage to legitimate and adopted children.[27]

The Tale of the Wives[28]

The deceased married his first wife years before he entered into a contractual union with his second wife. It was not possible to have the contractual union solemnized and registered. The deceased had not made a Will before his death and so intestate laws applied. After his death, his second "wife" claimed that her three children were lawful children of the deceased and hence were each entitled to a share in his estate. The first wife then brought proceedings against the second wife, refuting her claims.

The court decided that the three children were not entitled to the deceased's estate as the children of the second "marriage" were unfortunately considered illegitimate. This case reflects the intention of the Women's Charter to abolish the institution of polygamy.

The circumstances in the illustration above are unlikely to occur in modern Singapore because there are now clear marriage records to ensure a second marriage is not registered. Nonetheless, the law stated in the case above has

---

[27] Intestate Succession Act (Cap. 146, 2013 Rev Ed) s 3 & s 7.
[28] *Re Estate of Liu Sinn Min* [1975] 1 MLJ 145.

still not been overruled. As a result, an illegitimate child would not be likely to receive any assets unless expressly provided for in the parent's Will. Essentially, the law of intestate succession does not work to an illegitimate child's benefit. He or she is treated as any other stranger in the eyes of the law with regards to succession unless express provision is made in the parent's Will.

As previously mentioned, the law generally favours the mother's involvement in the life of an illegitimate child. Yet, an illegitimate child would only have an interest in his or her mother's intestate estate where there is no legitimate child surviving the mother.[29]

Another issue with illegitimate children is that an illegitimate child is unable to apply for maintenance from the parent's estate following the parent's death.[30] The reference to children in the Inheritance (Family Provision) Act does not expressly include illegitimate children. Consequently, the court has held that illegitimate children are not qualified to apply to court for maintenance to be provided by their deceased parent's estate.[31] However, in the aforesaid case the court also added that reforms were necessary as it would be unfair to punish innocent children who have no control over their legitimacy.

Note the difference between an application by an illegitimate child for maintenance from the deceased parent's estate and maintenance from a living parent. A living parent is required under law to maintain his/her child.

Maintenance of an Illegitimate Child

If you are a parent, you will have an ongoing duty to provide for your child, regardless of whether the child is legitimate or illegitimate.[32] This is because the law recognises the responsibility of a parent to contribute to the maintenance of his child in any circumstance.

Factors similar to the ones mentioned in the preceding paragraphs relating to legitimate children also apply in the assessment of the quantum of maintenance to be provided for illegitimate children.

---

[29] Leong Wai Kum, Elements of Family Law in Singapore (LexisNexis, 2012) at p 74.

[30] Inheritance (Family Provision) Act (Cap. 138, 1985 Rev Ed) s 3(1).

[31] *AAG v Estate of AAH, deceased* [2010] 1 SLR 769; [2009] SGCA 56.

[32] *Supra* n 20, at s 68.

Chapter Six

The Misstep: Divorce

I hardly said a word to my wife until I said 'yes' to divorce.
— *John Milius & Franas Coppola*

Once the wedding dress is hung up and the confetti swept away, newlyweds are left to deal with the idiosyncrasies of life as a married couple. Expectations may not meet reality and this may then potentially lead to areas of conflict in a marriage. Instances of discord, if not addressed and solved either internally or via marriage counselling, may then escalate to divorce.

Deciding to get a divorce is a major life decision. There are many consequences which may last a lifetime. Many a time, it affects not just the couple but also the people who love and care for them. The divorce process is often the last resort for an unhappy marriage. Yet, the number of divorces and annulments in Singapore has been increasing in real terms over the past few years.[1] Specifically, there were 7,604 divorces and annulments recorded in 2011, an increase from the figure of 6,904 in 2006.[2]

Unfortunate as it sounds, couples must be aware that the eventuality of divorce is a possibility and be mindful that this Damocles sword hangs

---

[1] *Key Indicators on Marriages and Divorces, 2006–2011*, Statistics Singapore.
[2] *Ibid.*

over every marriage. This chapter addresses the potential areas for conflict in marriage, marriage counselling, grounds for divorce, custody battles, maintenance and division of assets.

MENDING MARRIAGES

A happy marriage is a long conversation that always seems too short.
— *Andres Maurois*

Frustration with one's partner is inevitable in a marriage. Often, the bigger sources of marital conflict may relate to money issues, in-laws, sexual relations or lack thereof with the spouse, and the bringing up of children.

However, the key to a successful marriage is to handle these conflicts with maturity and love. Both partners must be careful not to let the conflicts interfere with an otherwise healthy and loving relationship. It helps to be able to pick up on hints in their daily lives and to act to resolve conflicts expeditiously.

Spotting the Signs

Petty strifes between couples may often mask a brewing displeasure concerning a certain habit, disposition or mannerism of the other. When two people live together under the same roof, it is sometimes the smallest of personality differences that may cause the most disproportionate outbursts. Often, a partner fails to get away with offensive acts and speech that a stranger can. Familiarity may cultivate an attitude of nonchalance towards each other.

But what if the partner is acting that way but not out of free will? The spotlight of this section is placed on mental illnesses, especially because these are traits that may potentially cause continuing conflicts.

Mental Illnesses

It has been reported in some jurisdictions that one in three people experience some form of mental illness at some point in their life.[3] In a recent survey,

---

[3]WHO International Consortium in Psychiatric Epidemiology, "Cross-national comparisons of the prevalences and correlates of mental disorders" (2000) Bulletin of the World Health Organization, Vol. 78, No. 4, p 416.

Major Depressive Disorder (MDD), Alcohol Abuse and Obsessive Compulsive Disorder (OCD) were found to be Singapore's three most common mental illnesses.[4] According to this survey, one in sixteen in Singapore had suffered from MDD at some point in their life.[5] For people in Singapore affected by Alcohol Abuse and OCD, the findings of the survey were one in twenty nine, and one in thirty three respectively. Fortunately, the figures are less worrying than they sound. Mental illnesses encompass a wide range of diseases and disorders. Examples include delusion, schizophrenia, eating disorders such as anorexia or bulimia, insomnia, personality disorders such as narcissism or antisocial or borderline personality disorder, OCD, depression and bipolar disorder.[6] Also, they vary in severity.

When a spouse displays recurrent erratic behaviour, the spontaneous reaction of the other may be to retaliate or to blame him or her for acting out. However, the spouse on the receiving end should keep in mind that this behaviour could merely be a symptom of a mental condition that the other spouse may not be aware of. If the spouse were to restrain the urge to reciprocate with like unreasonableness, and instead explore the possibility of the other acting this way as a result of a mental condition, the spouse may be able to get to the root of the problem.

Of course, detecting signs of mental illness especially if not severe or easily noticeable, is never an easy task. More often than not, while the symptoms of any health condition may be easily identifiable in theory, it may take a great deal of personal attention or even an expert's opinion for a mental illness to be detected. Thankfully, the familiarity and close interaction between spouses place a spouse in a relatively better position to spot any telltale signs of a psychiatric ailment. It also provides opportunities for careful persuasion by a spouse, such that the sufferer willingly seeks qualified medical diagnosis and treatment.

The actions and responses of both parties to the illness may break or strengthen a relationship. If a person suffering from a mental condition chooses to ignore signs and refuses medical help, this may have disastrous

---

[4]*Latest study sheds light on the state of mental health in Singapore*, 18 November 2011, available at <www.imh.com.sg>.
[5]*Ibid.*
[6]This list has been adapted from <www.silverribbonsingapore.com>.

effects on the person, the couple's relationship and the family unit as a whole. In these cases, it is advisable that the other spouse be tolerant, but act immediately if he or she honestly thinks there is more to the unreasonable behaviour than meets the eye. Misunderstandings may breed issues of trust and disrupt the balance of harmony within the family unit. Furthermore, it is more likely than not that untreated mental disorders may persist for a long time if left untreated.

It is for these reasons that the somewhat awkward yet daunting task of suggesting treatment or at least professional counselling should be done at the earliest. Living with a mentally ill spouse is challenging, but with professional help, a partner can better understand the mental condition to exercise greater patience with his or her mentally ill spouse. It also helps if the partner can confide in family, friends and colleagues about the illness and receive moral support to cope with it. Yet mental illness still carries a social stigma in our society and this deters both the sufferers and their families from getting the professional help they need and there is a tendency to cover up instead.

On the bright side, more and more Singaporeans are perhaps drawing away from the narrow-minded view of the mentally ill as "crazy people". In the past, many sufferers chose to refrain from seeking help to avoid the social stigma associated with mental illnesses. However, with consistent effort being put into educating the public, there is now a greater awareness of the physiological aspect of mental illness and society is beginning to understand that having a mental illness is a health condition that may happen to anyone, regardless of status, race, language or religion.

Mental illness is not an automatic ground for divorce in Singapore. This in itself is a spouse's reminder of the vow to stay married "in sickness and in health". Nonetheless, because mental sickness often gives rise to erratic behaviour, they could become catalysts to a divorce filed on the grounds of unreasonable behaviour. An illustration of this would be where the mentally ill spouse poses a danger to the children or to those around him or her.

Postpartum Depression

Postpartum depression is a mental condition more commonly known as postnatal depression. This is caused by a change in the woman's hormonal levels after childbirth.

When a woman becomes pregnant, doctors may warn her loved ones to be on the alert for signs of prenatal depression. The depression could continue or even escalate after the child is born. Yet, in coping with the excitement and flurry of activities that a new addition to the family brings, it is easy for the rest of the family to overlook the new mother's emotional well-being.

Statistics show that postpartum depression affects approximately 10–15% of the women in Singapore after childbirth.[7] The following is a non-exhaustive list of symptoms that may reflect postpartum depression:

- The mother has lost her sense of humour.
- The mother appears disinterested in activities she used to look forward to.
- There are instances where the mother condemns herself unnecessarily.
- The mother appears jittery and worried for no good reason.
- There are nights where the mother has had difficulty sleeping.
- The mother expresses the thought of harming herself or has been caught doing so.[8]

Early identification and intervention is crucial in helping mothers recover from postnatal depression. The list only serves as a guide. Signs and symptoms of postnatal depression are often almost imperceptible and can occur slowly over time.

It is not uncommon for couples to encounter hiccups in their marriages after the birth of their child. Unhappy husbands often lament that their wives are no longer the woman they married years ago. However, what they may not realise is that the changes in her behaviour could be the result of postnatal depression. If postnatal depression is left unidentified and untreated, the husband may hold his wife's behaviour against her without knowing that she could be ill. This may then sow the seed for further disagreements in the years to come. It is thus crucial for a husband to be extremely vigilant and sensitive to the possibility that his wife may be suffering from postnatal depression.

Naturally, new mothers must also play their part in monitoring their mental health. Although this may seem a daunting task for the new mother, informing

---

[7] This data on postnatal depression and its statistics can be found on the SingHealth website at <www.singhealth.com.sg>.

[8] This list has been adapted from the Edinburgh Postnatal Depression Scale given in J.L. Cox, J.M. Holden and R. Sagovsky, (1987) *British Journal of Psychiatry*, Vol. 150.

her better half is always a good start. Conquering these fears together as a couple is what makes a relationship what it is — a trusting union and a safe shelter.

If a new mother exhibits similar characteristics as those given in the list, it is highly advisable that she seeks or is persuaded to seek professional and medical help expediently. Often, the husband and other family members ought to take the lead since they are in a better position to detect these behaviour patterns.

Menopause

Menopause is a normal part of any woman's life and would typically occur during her 40s or 50s. This marks a time of transition from a period of fertility to the end of the fertile phase of a woman.

The symptoms of menopause are exhibited by the body as a response to fluctuating levels of hormones. Responses vary from woman to woman and accordingly, some experience symptoms for months while others have symptoms that last for five years or more; some women may not experience any visible signs while others may react extremely.[9] In most cases, these manifestations are natural and expected.

Without acknowledging the implications of menopause, the transition may put a strain on a couple's loving relationship. It is therefore highly advisable that the woman's loved ones, particularly her husband, deals with these symptoms patiently and considerately. As a woman goes through menopause, there are three general areas that may change.

The first change may be physical. As the female body undergoes transition, many women undergo physical changes such as weight gain, hot flashes and/or hair loss. Some may suffer from body aches and stiffness in their joints. A decreased libido may also make the wife feel less attractive. All these factors may accumulate to affect the wife's self-esteem negatively and the spousal relationship as a whole.

---

[9]More information on menopause can be found on the SingHealth website at <www.singhealth.com.sg>.

The second change may be emotional. A woman may experience severe mood swings, anxiety, depression, panic attacks, and increased irritability. With hormones raging out of control, she may be confused and upset at the slightest change of plans. It is usually then up to the family and the loving spouse to exercise patience and care in understanding her inability to control her emotions.

The third change may be spiritual or soulful. Often, women who undergo menopause reach a stage in life where their children are sufficiently old to take care of themselves and they or their husbands may already be at the peak of their careers, with nothing particularly new or exciting to look forward to. For these women, life takes them on a new journey of self-discovery or a new focus that may come in the form of a new hobby or activity which may disrupt the routine of family life. This may inevitably affect the couple's relationship and the status quo of the family unit.

No matter what the symptoms or effects of menopause are, menopause cannot be prevented. It is therefore up to the couple to decide whether this challenging phase of life serves to strengthen their relationship or tears them apart.

Finding the Solution

Marriage counselling is one of the many avenues open for couples at any stage of their marriage. Regardless of the extent of acrimony, it is never too late to seek appropriate help. The fire in the relationship can die down but the embers may continue to glow. Counselling can help spark the same embers and re-ignite the fire that led them to marry each other in the first place.

Professional help may be sought from many places including many government-linked Family Service Centres or privately owned counselling centres. Religion-based marital counselling is also available to willing couples at various religious centres or places of worship.

Attending the sessions with an open mind will facilitate the work of the marriage counsellor. A third-party listener is always helpful in obtaining an objective new outlook on the situation. Ultimately, counselling serves as a gentle reminder of why the couple took the plunge to marry. A neutral party helps to unmask the loving and trusting foundation on which the relationship had been built and upon which the relationship continues to stand, amidst the stress of everyday life.

Integrative Behavioural Couple Therapy

Integrative Behavioural Couple therapy is a rather new approach to couple therapy that is still being researched and developed. Its concept, based on mutual reciprocity and reinforcement, encourages healthy interaction between the couples through better communication and reversal of negative thought patterns. Behavioural therapy also teaches spouses to manage their conflicts in a calm and mature way.

This therapy is groundbreaking as it integrates acceptance and change as well as a variety of treatment strategies within the therapy process. Usually, there are two phases to this process. First, an evaluation or feedback stage where the therapist learns of the couple's concerns, struggles and the history of their relationship. At this stage, the couple provides their typical reactions to a variety of spousal situations and corrects the therapist's impressions when he or she gets it wrong.

The second would be the active treatment phase. The focus here may be on a recent event or events that have triggered quarrels or disagreements. The couple is made to act out the situation or describe their behaviour in words. During these sessions, the therapist helps the partners speak about their emotions and aspirations in an open manner and facilitates the search for alternative ways of interaction and behaviour by dismissing negative thoughts and emotive patterns. Exercises and training are conducted to acquire positive thought processes and habits in their place.

Rather than purely talking and mulling over spousal issues, this therapeutic technique requires active involvement of both spouses to deal with their problem or problems. The goal here is for the pair to recognise patterns of behaviour or thought that are the root of their clashes, and to learn how to break these patterns. In this way, the participating spouse is more equipped to reach amicable resolutions by focusing on what he or she can do in the marriage rather than what the other spouse cannot.

Parenting Programme

A couple may be required to complete a parenting programme before they will be allowed to file for divorce, which will provide information on matters relating to marriage, divorce and how a divorce may affect children. Where the court considers it to be in the interests of the parties or their children, it may also direct either or both parties to complete a parenting programme at any stage of the proceedings.[10]

Counselling and Mediation for Divorcing Couples with Children

The law makes it mandatory for couples with any child below 21 years old to go for counselling and/or mediation after their divorce is filed. It is also possible that the court orders the children to attend counselling sessions with their parents.[11] In instances where the court considers it to be in the interests of the parties and their children, it may direct that the parties or their children attend mediation or counselling or to participate in family support programmes instead, even before the divorce proceedings are heard.[12] This is to allow couples to understand better the effect the divorce might have on their children, as well as on the family unit as a whole and to assist the children in addressing their concerns and fears regarding the pending divorce. Either option can help to resolve any manifest familial issues in an amicable fashion for the benefit of the children in the long run. The court will arrange the scheduling of these sessions, the type and frequency of which will be determined in view of the circumstances. However, the court may exempt the couple or their children from attending such sessions if it considers them not to be in their interest.[13] Nonetheless, it is recommended that couples go for counselling as a preventive measure, rather than wait for divorce proceedings to begin before attending counselling.

---

[10]New Section 94A of the Women's Charter enacted by the Women's Charter (Amendment) Act 2016 which comes into effect in October 2016.

[11]According to Women's Charter (Cap. 353, 2009 Rev Ed) s 50(3A). This applies to couples who have filed for divorce on or after 1 October 2014 and have at least one child who is below 21 years old when proceedings are commenced. See, Women's Charter (Mediation and Counselling) (Prescribed Persons) (Amendment) Rules 2014 r 2(1).

[12]Amendment of Section 50(2) of the Women's Charter enacted by the Women's Charter (Amendment) Act 2016 which comes into effect in October 2016.

[13]*Id*, at s 50(3B).

Marriage counselling in all its different permutations should always be seen as an option for couples stuck in a temporary phase of difficulty. It is through a calm and controlled airing of grievances that a couple can more easily perfect the tricky balancing of two distinct personalities.

GROUNDS FOR DIVORCE

In every marriage more than a week old, there are grounds for divorce. The trick is to find, and continue to find, grounds for marriage.

— Robert Anderson

Not every unhappily married couple can get a divorce granted by the court. There are certain legal requirements that must be met before a divorce is granted.

First, the marriage must have at least lasted three years.[14] That is to say no divorce application may be brought unless three years have passed since the date of solemnization of marriage. This deters people from jumping into a marriage without serious thought. The rule also has its roots in public policy to ensure that couples have taken adequate time to attempt to reconcile in a bid to save their marriage.

However, the law makes an exception where there is exceptional hardship suffered by one party or exceptional depravity displayed by the other.[15]

The Runaway Wife[16]

N was 42 years old and hoped to start a family of his own. Through a marriage agency, he entered into an arranged marriage with a 21-year-old

---

[14]*Id*, at s 94(1).
[15]*Id*, at s 94(2).
[16]*Ng Kee Shee v Fu Gaofei* [2005] 4 SLR(R) 762; [2005] SGHC 171.

woman. However, after the marriage, she constantly refused intimacy with N. Staying over at her friend's house was a frequent occurrence and on one occasion, she even refused to get into the same car as N. Five months later, she finally returned to China and never came back to Singapore. In a phone call to N, the wife told him that the marriage was a mistake and that she would rather die than return to him.

The court found that N had entered into the marriage whole-heartedly and had even begged his spouse to return. On the other hand, it was the wife who had absolutely no regard for the marriage and who had entered into the marriage impulsively. Since she had clearly stated that she would never return to N, there was nothing left in the marriage to salvage. Hence, to force N to wait for the three year time-bar to expire would be to make him pay for his wife's wrongdoing. N was granted a divorce even though the marriage lasted less than three years.

Second, the court must be satisfied that the marriage has broken down irretrievably[17] such that the circumstances make it just and reasonable to grant a divorce to the Plaintiff.[18] To show that a marriage is beyond repair, the spouse applying for a divorce must show one or more of the following:[19]

- Adultery by the Defendant;
- Behaviour that makes it unreasonable for the Plaintiff to continue living with the Defendant (commonly referred to as "unreasonable behaviour").
- Desertion lasting for a continuous period of at least 2 years immediately preceding the filing of the writ;
- Separation for three consecutive years, and the Defendant consents to the divorce (commonly referred to as "divorce with consent"); or
- Separation for four consecutive years (commonly referred to as "divorce without consent").

---

[17]*Supra* n 10, at s 95(1).
[18]*Supra* n 10, at s 95(2).
[19]*Supra* n 10, at s 95(3).

These grounds for divorce will be elaborated below in turn. Here, the "Plaintiff" refers to the spouse bringing the divorce proceedings to court and seeking a divorce while the "Defendant" refers to the spouse being sued. For convenience, the terms are retained even if both parties are willing to dissolve their marriage. The Plaintiff is usually the party that files the divorce application and serves the required court documents on the other spouse first.

Adultery

The court may grant the Plaintiff a divorce if the Defendant has committed adultery with another person and the Plaintiff can adduce evidence to show that he or she finds it intolerable to live with the Defendant because of the Defendant's adultery. A person cannot rely on his or her own acts of adultery to obtain a divorce.

It is not particularly difficult for a person's actions to be considered adulterous. If a married person voluntarily engages in consensual sexual intercourse with anyone other than his or her spouse, that person commits adultery. However, the court will not merely rely on the testimony of the spouse who has been cheated on without any proof.

The Plaintiff may prove adultery in inter alia, the following ways:

1. The Defendant confesses to committing adultery.
2. A witness who personally witnessed the sexual intercourse comes forward to testify.
3. Where it can be inferred from circumstances that adultery has been committed and there is no other inference that can be made from that set of circumstances. Spouses can produce such evidence with the help of private investigators who can assist in providing circumstantial evidence, which would include photos, videos and testimony. However, for the reports provided by private investigators to be used as evidence in court, it must be obtained *before* any divorce proceedings are commenced.
4. A child borne of the couple is proven not to be of the male Plaintiff.[20] Divorce applications made on the ground that the child is not his child will

---

[20]In some cases, the birth certificate of the child borne out of an adulterous relationship may be produced where the Plaintiff is not named as the parent.

be heard by the court. Evidence such as DNA test reports can be adduced to prove paternity and to rebut the presumption that the husband is the father of the child borne during the marriage or within 280 days after its dissolution, the mother remaining unmarried.[21]

Love's Not A Competition (But I'm Winning)[22]

Mr and Mrs E were struggling in their marriage. Both parties accused each other of having love affairs and questionable morals.

Mrs E claimed that Mr E actively engaged in pornography at home, including frequently visiting pornographic websites on their home computer. He even committed adultery while she was pregnant with their child. Subsequently in their marriage, Mr E admitted to the affair but blamed it on intoxication and the seductress.

According to Mr E, his wife became violent after the confession. He claimed that she would beat and scratch him. He also alleged that Mrs E was promiscuous and had an extramarital affair while she was still married. To support his case, he added that she also had an affair with her Caucasian boss and behaved intimately with other male friends.

The court heard evidence from both sides and concluded that Mr E had exaggerated his claims about his wife. The court then concluded that the marriage be dissolved based on the unreasonable behaviour of the husband. However the court declared that neither party won or lost all their issues. As a result, the court ordered each party to pay their own lawyers' and court fees.

In the case above, evidence of both adultery and unreasonable behaviour were put forward. Yet, the court only elected a single ground for divorce. Generally, where there are few grounds of divorce, the judge will go for the

---

[21] Status of Children (Assisted Reproduction Technology) Act 2013 s 16 (amending s 114 of the Evidence Act) which allows, subject to the provisions under the Status of Children (Assisted Reproduction Technology) Act 2013, the presumption of paternity to be displaced if it is proven otherwise.

[22] *EY v EZ* [2004] SGDC 91.

strongest qualifying ground that was proven by evidence. Here, the stronger case was made for unreasonable behaviour.

Unreasonable to Expect Continual Cohabitation

This limb is colloquially called "unreasonable behaviour". However, the court does not merely look for unreasonable behaviour alone when evaluating an application based on this particular ground of divorce.

The key issue the court has to determine is whether given the facts of the case, including the history of the marriage, the couple's relationship, their individual traits and personalities, the conduct of the Defendant has affected the particular Plaintiff to the extent that the Plaintiff cannot reasonably be expected to live with the Defendant.[23] In making such assessment, the court's primary focus is not on the culpability of the Defendant's conduct but rather the cumulative effects of the Defendant's conduct, both passive and active, on the particular Plaintiff. These may include a spouse's refusal to have sex with the Plaintiff[24] or a spouse's act of violence which endangers the personal health or safety of others.[25]

This is the most commonly used ground for divorce, probably because of its all-encompassing nature. The provision is able to accommodate an extremely wide array of scenarios.

Desertion for 2 Years

If the Defendant has deserted the Plaintiff for a continuous period of at least two years immediately preceding the filing of the writ, the court may grant the Plaintiff a divorce.

Desertion is a rather legal term but simply put, it essentially consists of two aspects.[26] First, both spouses must live separately. Second, there must be an intention by the deserting spouse to abandon his or her spouse. Desertion is different from separation, as separation is designed only as temporary

---

[23]*Wong Siew Boey v Lee Boon Fatt* (1994) 1 SLR(R) 323.

[24]*Castello Ana Paula Costa Fusillier v Lobo Carlos Manuel Rosado* [2003] 4 SLR 331.

[25]*Sundari Raja Singam v Rasaratnam Raja Singam* [1974–1976] SLR(R) 624.

[26]*Perry v Perry* (1952) P 203 (Court of Appeal) per Evershed MR.

relief for the spouses. Further, when a couple separates, either party can commence divorce proceedings. However, for desertion, only the deserted party can bring the action.

In order to form an intention to desert, the Defendant must intend to bring the matrimonial union to a permanent end. It must not be consensual and the Defendant must leave the marriage without having any good reason to do so. If the Defendant received and fulfilled an overseas posting for work or had to go abroad for health reasons, these periods of time during which the couple lived apart do not constitute desertion and will not be considered in assessing the occurrence of desertion.

Separation with or without Consent

An irretrievable breakdown of marriage can be shown by the Plaintiff if the spouses have lived apart for a continuous period of at least four years. In this scenario, the Defendant does not have to consent to the divorce. He or she does however have the opportunity to contest the divorce petition, for example, where he or she disagrees with what is said in the divorce writ.

If the Plaintiff requests a divorce on the grounds of separation and the Defendant consents to the divorce, the spouses only need to have lived apart for a continuous period of three years before the filing of the petition to qualify for divorce.

However, physical separation is not the only consideration in either case. Even if a couple lives apart, the law may not necessarily find that there was separation.

> ### Getting a Clean Break[27]
>
> After living apart for four years, Mr L applied to the court to obtain a divorce from his wife Mrs L. This story, however, had a twist. Although Mr L did not sleep at his matrimonial home for four years, he would continue to do the things he would normally have done had he remained

---

[27] *Leong Kwek Keong v Lee Ying Kuan* [1990] 1 SLR(R) 112; [1990] SGHC 8.

at home. Mr L returned home every day to spend time with his family, he ate dinners at home and Mrs L would wash and iron his clothes for him. He also continued to have sexual intercourse with Mrs L, as if they were still married. In fact, Mrs L became pregnant with his child two years after they had started living apart.

The court decided that living apart required something more than just living in separate beds. One or both the spouses must form the intention to dissociate from the relationship and act as if the marital relationship has been severed. In this case, although Mr L did not physically sleep in the matrimonial home every night, he spent almost all his non-working and non-sleeping hours with his family. As a result, their divorce was not granted.

Conversely, a couple could still be considered to be "living apart" even if they stayed under the same roof. What really matters is whether or not the couple continues to live as if they were one household.

Allowances for Reconciliation

Marriage requires romance but it also takes commitment and hard work from both partners. It would therefore not be surprising that the daily grind of day-to-day life could result in friction in a marriage. Rather than to muffle abrasion with the old saying *"Time heals what reason cannot"*, an ideal solution is for parties to attempt to resolve their troubles as they come.

Yet, time is a significant element considered by the courts in determining whether a particular marriage has broken down irretrievably. For example, as was mentioned previously, in a divorce based on consent of the Defendant, separation must last for at least three years before it qualifies to be used as a basis for divorce. Reasonably, spouses may be deterred from resuming cohabitation so as to avoid disrupting the period of separation.

To encourage spouses to work through their troubles together, the law provides for a period of six months that allows for attempts at reconciliation to be made before a divorce writ is filed.[28] Attempts may include the couple living together again and participating in leisurely activities as spouses.

As previously described, if adultery is the ground of the divorce proceedings, the Plaintiff must prove two elements — the Defendant's adultery and the Plaintiff finding that it is intolerable to live with the Defendant because of his or her adultery. The court chooses to disregard up to six months of cohabitation that occurs after the Plaintiff knows of the infidelity. This period is taken as the spouses' attempt at reconciliation and will not be factored in when the court determines whether the Plaintiff finds it intolerable to live with his or her spouse. However, living together beyond the span of six months after the last act of adultery bars the use of infidelity as a ground for divorce.

In cases where unreasonable behaviour is relied upon as the ground for divorce, cohabitation up to six months will be disregarded in determining whether parties can reasonably be expected to keep living together. In such a case, the relevant period of up to six months will be excluded after the date of the occurrence of the final incident relied on by the Plaintiff (and upheld by the court to support the allegation of unreasonable behaviour) and until the date when the divorce writ is filed.

Finally, for the ground of desertion or separation, any cohabitation up to six months or less will be similarly disregarded. This rule has been adopted even though parties are required to live apart for at least two years in the case of desertion before a divorce writ can be filed. However, any period up to a maximum of six months, during which the parties lived together, cannot be factored in the minimum required period for filing a divorce writ based on desertion or separation.

In all the above four cases, the calculation of the six-month period does not require the cohabitation to be continuous.[29] For instance, three attempts at cohabitation lasting two months each and spanning across a period of two years would still satisfy the six-month rule.

---

[28] A divorce writ is filed at the first stage of divorce. That is to say, you apply for a divorce by filing a writ for divorce and related papers.

[29] *Supra* n 10, at s 95(5)–(7).

A Final Note

Generally, the court will strive to protect the interests of the child. The court may refuse or delay granting a judgment of divorce until the child is prepared to handle the confusion and trauma of the family breakup. This is because the court recognises that divorce affects not just the parents but the entire family unit.[30]

In conclusion, the court will typically refuse to grant the judgment of divorce until it finds that the marriage has already broken down irretrievably, and that a grant of divorce in the particular case would be just and reasonable.

DIVORCE HEARINGS

The entire divorce process comprises two stages.

The first stage is complete when Interim Judgment is given and the second (and final) stage is complete after all the ancillary issues are settled. The divorce procedure is outlined below.[31]

The first stage begins with the filing of the divorce writ. The couple then goes through divorce proceedings where an Interim Judgment would be granted if the judge is satisfied that the marriage has irretrievably broken down.

However, even after the Interim Judgment has been given, in reality, many issues remain unresolved as an Interim Judgment is meant only as a provisional order for divorce.

The next stage of the divorce process thus concentrates on the settlement of these ancillary issues. These ancillary issues may comprise the care, custody and control of children, the division of the matrimonial assets and maintenance orders for the ex-wife, incapacited ex-husband and children.

Before ancillary matters are heard in the court, parties have to declare their assets in order for the court to make a fair assessment of the case. As part of this declaration made, the parties will also be asked to submit their proposed plans for the living arrangements of their children if there are any, and for the determination of any outstanding financial issues. Parties

---

[30]*Id*, at s 95(4).

[31]More information can also be found on the State Courts of Singapore website at <www.statecourts.gov.sg>.

are strongly encouraged to be upfront and honest in declaring their assets because the court will view any concealment of assets in a negative light.

Where's My Money?[32]

Over the span of a marriage lasting twenty-three years, a whole array of matrimonial assets were accumulated. This included the estranged couple's matrimonial home, country club memberships, two Mercedes Benz cars, their respective cash assets and CPF savings, and several companies incorporated and developed during the marriage.

However, the court found that the husband had not been completely honest in disclosing all his personal assets. The large discrepancy in his declared assets was approximately $2.7m. Yet, he failed to provide a sensible explanation for the omission.

The court drew an adverse inference that he had more assets than what was declared and awarded his wife a larger portion than what she would have received if the husband had been forthcoming.

Neither party can remarry until the Interim Judgment has been made final. This is when a Certificate of Making Interim Judgment Final is issued by the court. This will conclude the divorce. In the following sections, we will discuss the main contentious issues that arise within each of these ancillary matters.

CHILDREN IN DIVORCE

As marriage is seen as an equal co-operative partnership in Singapore, both husband and wife have a legal duty to care and provide for their child as best as they can.[33]

While financial assets of a marriage can be divided and apportioned in a clear-cut manner, it is impossible to do the same for child-related concerns. Often, both parents are willing to spend much time, effort, energy and money

---

[32]*NK v NL* [2007] 3 SLR 743.
[33]*Supra* n 10, at s 46(1).

raising their child but unfortunately fail to agree on what is truly best for their child. Custody battles that are dramatised in movies are, in reality, emotionally and physically draining, pedantic and costly.

Custody

The term "custody" is commonly used when the guardianship of children is called into question. While this distinction is not made in the Women's Charter, the courts have clarified that 'custody' is a separate concept from 'care and control' of a child. Accordingly, a parent with custody of a child may not necessarily also have 'care and control'.[34] The child need not always stay with the parent who has custody. Neither does a grant of custody mean that the particular parent is the maker of all decisions relating to the child, be it major or minor.

Legally, having custody over a child allows the parent to make major decisions regarding the upbringing of the child. In practical terms, this would include decisions in three major aspects of the child's life: education, religion, and health.

It is the norm for courts to order joint custody of the child.[35] This is because the court wishes to encourage both parents to continue to have a direct involvement in the child's life even after the divorce. A joint custody order thus serves as a reminder to parents to work together harmoniously to promote the child's best interests.

Exceptionally, a sole custody order is made. This may encompass situations where one parent had physically, sexually, or emotionally abused the child on previous occasion(s). Where the relationship between both parents is especially acrimonious and parental co-operation thought to be impossible, the courts may also award sole custody to one parent. This is because the court ultimately looks to safeguard the interests of the child. The parents' lack of co-operation might end up having an adverse impact on the child which the courts wish to avoid in the interests of the child.

---

[34] *CX v CY (minor: custody and access)* [2005] SGCA 37 at [30]–[35].
[35] *Id*, at [18].

Care and Control, and Access

As mentioned above, one crucial point to note is that custody is a separate concept from 'care and control' of the child. 'Care and control' is usually what is more hotly contested because this essentially decides who the child lives with.

That is to say, the parent who has care and control of the child has the authority to make the smaller decisions necessary for the child's ordinary day-to-day life. This may include matters such as the child's diet, the types of enrichment classes the child attends and whether or not the child is allowed to attend a sleepover party.

Sometimes Less is More[36]

Mr and Mrs A got married in 2000 and had a daughter eight years later. Unfortunately, their relationship had already deteriorated by then and one week before the birth of their daughter, the wife left the matrimonial home to live with her parents. As the relationship became more and more estranged, disagreements on how to bring up the child became progressively heated. It came to a head when both did not agree on which pre-school centre to send their daughter to and ended up sending her to both. This meant that the poor child had to attend one pre-school in the morning and another one in the afternoon. Mr A then appealed to the court for shared care and control of his daughter.

The court refused to grant shared care and control of the child to both parents because they had very different ideas on how to bring the child up. The court noted that if shared care and control were ordered, the young child would suffer unnecessary stress from having to adapt to unrealistic expectations of both parents. The court decided that it would be best for the young child to be provided with a constant routine and that the disruptions caused by the parents' acrimony would not be in the child's best interest.

In the end, Mrs A was given sole care and control. The court found that the infant had a closer relationship with her mother who was also

---

[36]*AQL v AQM* [2011] SGHC 264.

capable of providing a safe and loving environment for her daughter. Granting Mrs A sole care and control meant that Mrs A would have the authority to decide which preschool to send her daughter to. As such, the poor child no longer needed to attend two schools. To ensure that Mr A was kept a part of the child's life, he successfully obtained access rights of four hours every weekday and six hours on Saturdays.

A parent who is not granted care and control of the child is not excluded from the child's life altogether. This is because it is almost customary that the courts will then award that parent access rights as seen in the case study above. Access ensures that the child continues to enjoy the love of the parent that he or she is not living with. It basically provides the parent with visitation rights to the child. This order is at the wide discretion of the court and could include overnight or overseas access.

Flexibility of the Courts

The future is unpredictable as circumstances can change. Where necessary, any order made by the court can be altered, varied or discharged on application by either parent or an appointed guardian.[37] This includes changing the parent who has care and control of the child and changing the custody status from joint to sole, where relevant evidence is brought to prove the case of the parent wanting that change.

The Decision that Divided a Nation[38]

M was raised by her expatriate birth parents as a Roman Catholic in the late 1930s. It was after her father was captured as a Prisoner-of-War during World War II that M's mother was left to fend for herself and her six children.

---

[37] Guardianship of Infants Act (Cap. 122, 1985 Rev Ed) s 5.
[38] *Re Maria Huberdina Hertogh; Adrianus Petrus Hertogh & Anor v Amina Binte Mohamed & Ors* [1951] 17 MLJ 12.

This did not last long and subsequently, M was sent away to live with C, a family friend. For the next eight years, M was brought up in a Muslim environment, circumcised and became a practising Muslim. She was even renamed Nadra.

When the war ended, M's parents requested her return to Holland but both C and M refused, preferring that the girl stay in Malaya. This was what triggered the court proceedings for child custody brought by M's parents.

A myriad of considerations was reviewed by the Singapore court — M's welfare, both present and future, the receipt of a potentially better education and broadening of M's experiences stemming from a life spent in Holland, and optimistically, a stable and fulfilling familial life under the care of her biological parents.

The court acknowledged that M's biological father was in a prison camp when she had been given away and was hence unaware what had happened. M's biological father argued that he would not have allowed M to be adopted or given away if he had known. Since the law recognizes that a father has the right to bring up the child in the way which he thinks is in the best interests of the child and the court chooses not to interfere when it believes the father has acted with the child's best interests at heart, the court ordered for M's return to her birth parents in Holland.

This case study tells of the controversial custody battle of Maria Hertogh which sparked the infamous riots that lasted for days.

Many have since criticised the judgment as racist, arguing that the judge had insinuated that life in Holland would provide better opportunities for the child than life in Malaya. Ironically, Maria's subsequent life in Holland turned out rather tragic. She was known to have always lamented her miserable life in Holland and her departure from Malaya. In fact, decades later, she was brought to trial for, but found not guilty of, the attempted murder of her husband. Soon after, the couple got a divorce. Interestingly enough, the Dutch court noted her unusual childhood and background in its judgment and recognised that the court decision and the subsequent events may have been more traumatic for her than anyone realised.

The Singapore court could not have possibly envisaged how Maria's life would turn out at the point when it gave its judgment. Anyone would have found it hard to speculate what the future held for a child at the age of thirteen. This difficulty remains for all custody battles brought before the court and it is these complications that the law seeks to avoid by being more flexible with custody arrangements.

The flexibility allows judges to attach conditions to court orders relating to custody, care and control. Usually, conditions are attached where there is fear that the parent might refuse to comply with the court order.[39] An example would be a prohibition barring one parent from taking the child overseas if there is a risk the child would not be returned to his or her home in Singapore.

Additionally, the court chooses to consider a broad range of factors and conditions such as money, physical comfort, moral and even religious welfare. As a result, although there are some general principles that the courts apply in cases involving children, none of these are set in stone. Such flexibility is what enables the courts to reach decisions that are best suited to the circumstances before them.

Welfare of the Child is Paramount

In all cases concerning children, the court will take the interests and the welfare of the child as its 'first and paramount consideration'.[40] This allows the court a wide discretion to make any directions or orders as it deems fit.

Courts generally agree that it is beneficial for a child to remain in his or her present environment. This status quo usually means making as few changes as possible to what the child is used to at the time of the application.[41] Additionally, courts recognise the maternal bond between an infant or young child and his or her mother. Hence, if there is no special reason to pick one parent over the other, such as a severe illness or mental incapacity, the court would generally keep the infant or young child with his or her mother.[42]

Where and when the child is sufficiently mature, the court will consider the expressed wishes of the child.[43] Note that if there are allegations that the

---

[39] *Supra* n10, at s 126(1) and s 126(2A).

[40] *Supra* n 35, at s 3.

[41] *Lim Chin Huat Francis & Anor v Lim Kok Chye Ivan & Anor* [1999] 2 SLR(R) 392.

[42] *Soon Peck Wah v Woon Che Chye* [1997] SGCA 49.

[43] *Supra* n 10, at s 125(2).

child has been "brainwashed" to take sides with one parent, the court could call for the child to be helped by a social welfare officer. If threats against the child by the parent are proven, these may be construed against that errant parent.

International Custody

When a Singaporean marries a foreigner and the foreigner moves back to his or her home country after the divorce, different custody arrangements must be made to ensure both parents have reasonable and fair access to their child. To make this happen, the child may have to travel overseas periodically. Again, the court ultimately takes into account the welfare of the child as the paramount consideration.

Usually, the court will wait until the child is of certain maturity or age before allowing the child to travel overseas to visit the foreign parent.[44] To do so, the judge evaluates the child's maturity on a case-by-case basis and makes his orders accordingly.[45] The condition that one parent flies with the child can also be attached. This will normally be done unless or until the child is used to travelling overseas alone.[46]

Grants of overseas access are usually determined separately from grants of local access. Hence, overseas access will not prejudice the access allowed when the foreigner travels here to visit his or her child resident in Singapore.

The Early Traveller[47]

Mr C, a Dutch and Mrs C, a Singaporean got married and had a child together. After their divorce, Mr C requested for the child to be granted overseas access to the Netherlands to see his parents. He argued that the bond between grandparents and grandchild was strong and he did not

---

[44]*T v C* [2003] SGDC 304 at [20].

[45]*Id* which stated the the child would be allowed to travel at the age of 12 while *infra* n 45 stated the child would be allowed to travel at the age of 9.

[46]*IF v IG* [2005] SGDC 95.

[47]*CX v CY* [2005] 3 SLR(R) 690; [2005] SGCA 37.

want the divorce to affect it. Mrs C disagreed and was afraid Mr C would not bring their child back to Singapore.

The court decided that Mr C had always complied with court orders and was unlikely to abduct the child and keep the child in the Netherlands. Although overseas trips may be destabilising for a four-year-old child, the court decided that it would have been in the interest of the child to maintain his bond with his paternal grandparents.

In reaching a compromise, the court decided that the child would be able to go overseas to visit his paternal grandparents not more than once every six months and for no longer than 14 days each time, so long as a parent accompanied the child during the trips abroad. In addition to reach a compromise, Mr C who was then stationed in Thailand, was allowed access to his child during his visits to Singapore.

Custody battles are intensely fought albeit with the parents' best intentions. The courts recognise the strong emotional bond between a parent and the child. Hence, the courts have created a set of flexible rules to allow for a child's ever-changing needs. Ultimately the court accepts that the welfare of the child always has to be kept as the central focus.

DIVISION OF MATRIMONIAL ASSETS

The division of matrimonial assets usually becomes one of the most contentious issues in a divorce. This is because individual assets are often combined, and savings and expenses of each spouse are intertwined. Hence when the marriage ends, parties often cannot agree on how these assets should be divided fairly. Often, one spouse contributes a larger financial proportion to the household. During a divorce proceeding, the spouse may feel that it is unfair for him or her not to be compensated accordingly. However, the other spouse may argue that besides monetary contributions, there were other significant contributions made, such as doing household chores, or looking after the children. Fortunately, the law takes into account both monetary and non-monetary factors to try and determine a fair division of assets.

Women's Charter (Cap. 353)

> **Power of Court to Order Division of Matrimonial Assets**
>
> **112. — (1)** The court shall have power, when granting or subsequent to the grant of a judgment of divorce, judicial separation or nullity of marriage, to order the division between the parties of any matrimonial asset or the sale of any such asset and the division between the parties of the proceeds of the sale of any such asset in such proportions as the court thinks just and equitable.

The process of dividing the assets can be split into two stages:

1. Having received the respective declarations of assets from each party, the court will determine whether each of these assets can be considered a "matrimonial asset".
2. Once the matrimonial assets have been earmarked, the court will then determine how these assets can be divided between the ex-spouses in a fair manner.

Assets That May Be Divided

Once an asset is considered to be a "matrimonial asset", the court will have the power to divide that asset between the two parties.

Generally, matrimonial assets are assets acquired during the marriage. Assets located abroad are no exception.[48]

Where the assets are acquired by one party before the marriage, these assets will be up for division if the court is satisfied that they have been ordinarily used or enjoyed by the couple or their children, while the parties are residing together for shelter or transportation or for household, education recreational, social or aesthetic purposes or if they had been substantially improved by the other party or by both during the marriage.[49]

---

[48]*Yow Mee Lan v Chen Kai Buan* [2000] 2 SLR(R) 659.
[49]*Supra* n 10, at s 112(10).

A matrimonial asset, however, does not include any asset acquired by one spouse before or during marriage by way of gift or inheritance unless it is a matrimonial home or it has been substantially improved during the marriage by the other spouse or both spouses to the marriage.[50]

On the interpretation of "gift" the court had ruled that where one spouse gives the asset to the other and the asset does not originate from a third-party gift or inheritance, such "pure" inter-spousal gift is not a "gift" under the statutory provision and the asset remains a matrimonial asset up for division. This is in recognition of the original input made by the donor spouse in first acquiring the property. The "gift" of the asset to the other spouse does not take it out of the pool of matrimonial assets unless the court opines that the nature of the gift is very personal or sentimental or the value is *de minimis*.

On the other hand, if the origin of the asset is traced to a third-party gift or inheritance, the same falls within the definition of "gift". Likewise, an inter-spousal "re-gift" where an asset which has been acquired by one spouse by way of a third-party gift or inheritance is given to the other spouse is also held to be a "gift" under the statutory enactment. Such "gift" is not a matrimonial asset unless the court is satisfied that it has been used as a matrimonial home or it has been substantially improved during the marriage by the other spouse who is not the recipient of the gift or by both parties to the marriage. The rationale is to prevent unmerited gain benefiting the other spouse as this will not accord with the original intention of the donor of the gift.[51]

It is left to be seen how the law will evolve in the interpretation of the statutory provision on the definition of matrimonial asset, in particular, in determining when a pre-marital asset or that acquired by gift or inheritance from a third-party by one spouse before or during the marriage is translated into a matrimonial asset to be divided between the couple.

---

[50] *Ibid.*
[51] *Wan Lai Cheng v Quek Seow Kee* [2012] 4 SLR 405.

A Gutsy Marriage[52]

In the United States of America, a husband donated his kidney to his wife which saved her life. Instead of the romantic fairytale ending he expected, his wife returned home only to begin a relationship with another man. She then commenced divorce proceedings. Humiliated and angry, he demanded his kidney back. As donated organs are not categorised as marital assets, the court held that he was not entitled to get it back. He then asked for USD1.5 million. The court denied his claim as it was illegal to put a monetary value on a human organ.

Specifically, the matrimonial home, which is the "family residence" of the couple, will almost always form part of the matrimonial assets. Hence, even if a married couple owns multiple properties, the matrimonial home still occupies a special legal status and this would typically be regarded as the common residence of the parties.

The Fair Division

Once the matrimonial assets have been identified, the courts will then proceed to determine how these assets should be divided between the two ex-spouses in the manner that the court deems just and equitable.

To determine whether a division is fair, the court considers all relevant circumstances including all non-monetary contributions expended during the course of the marriage. This broad-brush approach is endorsed implicitly in the provisions of the Women's Charter.

Some of the factors considered by the court include:[53]

1. Contributions made by each party to acquire, improve or maintain the matrimonial assets;

---

[52]Larry McShane, "Long Island Doctor Richard Batista to Estranged Wife: Give me my kidney back or $1.5 m" *Daily News New York*, 7 January 2009.
[53]*Supra* n10, s 112(2), read with s 114(1).

2. Any debt owing or obligation incurred or undertaken by either party for their joint benefit or for the benefit of any child of the marriage;

3. The needs of the children (if any) of the marriage;

4. Contributions made by each party to the welfare of the family;

5. Any agreement between the parties made in contemplation of divorce;

6. Any period of rent-free occupation or other benefit enjoyed by one party in the matrimonial home to the exclusion of the other party; and/or

7. The giving of assistance or support by one party to the other party (whether or not of a material kind).

8. Relevant matters that the court takes into consideration in assessing maintenance.

Once the proportions have been determined, the details will then be worked out so that the division is achieved in the most expedient way possible. In doing so, the court has a wide discretion in the type of orders it chooses to grant. This may include an order for:

- sale with a division of the proceeds;
- a postponed sale; or
- a grant of occupancy to either party for such period and on such terms as the court thinks fit.[54]

This list is in no way exhaustive and the court may also choose to attach other conditions to the order where appropriate.

A Literal Divide[55]

A Cambodian couple were estranged. Instead of settling their divorce in court, the husband decided literally to split their assets in two. The husband and his friends moved all his belongings to one side of the house and sawed the property into two separate halves with chainsaws.

---

[54]*Id*, at s 112(5).

[55]A House Divided: Estranged Couple's Home Cut in Half, CNN, 9 October 2008. This story is reproduced for illustrative purposes only. It does not reflect or represent Singapore law.

Amazingly, both halves survived intact albeit precariously perched. He then transported his half of the house to his parents' property while the wife continued to reside in her half that was left standing. The half-building continues to be an interesting sight to behold in their village.

Once the orders for the division of matrimonial assets are made, the court will not lightly vary or revoke the same unless the orders cannot be carried out or they fail to provide for a certain contingency which has since arisen.[56]

The court may extend, vary, revoke or discharge any order made and subject to such terms and conditions as it deems fit.[57]

Spousal Agreements

Pre-nuptial agreements were previously mentioned in Chapter Two. These, along with post-nuptial agreements, which are agreements made after marriage, are entered into by the couple privately. Although it is likely that the terms contained in the agreement have already been thoroughly deliberated upon and there would likely be specific provisions on the division of assets in the event of a divorce, the court will not blindly enforce the spousal agreement when dividing matrimonial assets. Instead, the court takes into consideration the spousal agreement as a factor and may incorporate some of the provisions into the consent order, where reasonable.

Agreeing to Disagree[58]

Ms T and Mr N were a married couple on the verge of divorce when they decided to agree on a settlement agreement that dealt with the division of their matrimonial assets and other ancillary matters. During divorce proceedings, Ms T sought to enforce this spousal agreement.

---

[56]*DX v DY* [2004] SGDC 239.

[57]*Supra* n 10, at s 112(4); *CT v CU* [2004] SGDC 164.

[58]*Tan Siew Eng (alias Tan Siew Eng Irene) v Ng Meng Hin* [2003] 3 SLR(R) 474; [2003] SGHC 27.

The divorce proceedings intensified as the trial progressed. During the proceedings, Ms T's counsel verbally attacked the testimonies of various members of Mr N's family while Mr N's counsel argued that Ms T had gone back on her word and that consequently, both parties should not be bound by the spousal agreement.

Upon hearing the arguments brought forth by both sides, the judge decided in this case, that the terms in the spousal agreement were fair and ordered that they be followed where applicable.

MAINTENANCE

Divorce is the one human tragedy that reduces everything to cash.
— Rita Mae Brown

Maintenance is, in essence, financial support. This topic was previously discussed as a matter for spousal consideration during the marriage. Expectedly, maintenance takes a greater significance when a marriage breaks down. It determines the ongoing obligations a spouse is burdened with, even when past the subsistence of the union.

The court has the power to order the husband to pay regular maintenance to the ex-wife. The wife may also be ordered to pay regular maintenance to the ex-husband, if he is unable to maintain himself due to any illness or mental disability. While the court may require a husband to maintain his ex-wife, the corresponding obligation of a wife to her former husband only arises in the exceptional situation where he is incapacitated.[59] However, the court may order both parents to pay regular maintenance for their child in view of the parents' co-equal responsibility to maintain his or her child. Maintenance for an ex-spouse and for children operates on a separate basis.

---

[59]Amendment of Section 113 of the Women's Charter enacted by the Women's Charter (Amendment) Act 2016 which comes into effect in October 2016.

As with custody, care and control orders that have been discussed above, maintenance orders can be varied after they have been made. However, the applicant must show that there has been a material change in circumstances. This would include reasons such as the child reaching adulthood, a fall in income for the paying ex-spouse, the non-earning ex-spouse now receiving a steady income or a financially active ex-spouse securing a higher salary.

Maintenance of Former Spouses

Traditionally, the husband has a legal duty to maintain his former wife in the event of a divorce. This perhaps reflects the idea that the husband is the sole breadwinner of the family and thus in the event of a breakdown of marriage, the wife should be provided for financially. However, this notion may no longer hold true in our society today. Unlike the era when the Women's Charter was enacted where women were predominantly housewives dependent on the pecuniary support from their husbands, women today are more educated and are capable of being financially independent.

In cognizance of the progress made by women today, the law now extends spousal maintenance from the wife to her husband or former husband if the latter becomes incapacitated due to physical or mental disability or any illness which renders him unable and continues to be unable to maintain himself. This is a gradual shift towards gender neutrality.[60]

Interim Maintenance Orders

The term "interim" may not mean much to some. However, it is distinct from a maintenance order made following a divorce. The two should not be confused.

When the divorce is contested, there could be a long wait till the issues of asset division and maintenance are settled by the court. During this time, the court may order the husband to pay appropriate sums of money to the wife while she awaits for her case to be adjudicated by the court.[61] This is known as an interim maintenance order.

---

[60]Amendment of Section 121E of the Women's Charter enacted by the Women's Charter (Amendment) Act 2016 which comes into effect in October 2016.
[61]*Supra* n 10, at s 113.

The interim order is only a temporary measure intended to ensure that the wife or the incapacitated husband is adequately provided for until the relevant judgment and orders are given by the court. Hence, the interim order is often lower than the final order.

Following from the point that the two concepts are separate, the court is not bound by an existing interim order when determining the final order of maintenance.[62]

Maintenance Orders

The law now extends the making of maintenance orders to provide for incapacitated former husbands as well. The aims of the court in granting a final maintenance order go beyond the aims of an interim maintenance order. A final order is often used to balance any financial inequality that the former wife might have endured during the marriage. These sacrifices would include, for example, her having to give up her job to take care of the children, or declining a lucrative career opportunity overseas to continue living with the family in Singapore. Likewise, the type of maintenance order to be given in favour of an incapacitated former husband would likely depend on the financial capability of the wife, his medical condition and necessities, and other circumstances of the case.

Because assets are of considerably higher monetary value, the court often chooses to decide on the issue of asset division before the issue of maintenance. If the court considers that there are insufficient assets to divide between the couple, it could then use the maintenance order to make up for any discrepancies or any financial inequality between the former spouses. This is because the maintenance order allows for future provision to be made. For example, if there is an existing order to divide assets, the amount of maintenance awarded may be reduced. In that sense, maintenance and asset division orders are seen to complement each other and each is determined with consideration made for the other.

This consideration is supplemented with many other factors the courts consider in determining the issue of maintenance to be given to the former wife or the incapacitated former husband. These may include the financial

---

[62]*Lee Bee Kim Jennifer v Lim Yew Khang Cecil* [2005] SGHC 209.

resources and needs of each ex-spouse, the standard of living enjoyed before the divorce, the parties' age and the duration of their marriage.[63] Essentially, all circumstances of the case will be considered relevant in coming to a judicial decision as to the type and quantum of maintenance payment to be awarded.[64]

The court first determines the type of maintenance order to be given. The order could be for periodic maintenance or a lump sum. The logic behind giving a lump sum order is to enable parties to achieve a clean break from each other.[65] If the husband is able to afford the lump sum and there is no continuing need to ensure that the wife is provided for, a lump sum order may be practical. Alternatively, if the parties are very acrimonious and hostile towards each other, the court may accept that it is more reasonable for a clean break.

In reality, the grant of a periodic maintenance order is more common. This imposes a continuing obligation on the former husband to pay his ex-wife a sum of monies that can be lowered or raised in future.

Typically, the court awards maintenance or does not award any maintenance at all. The difference between the two is that an award for maintenance carries with it the option of applying for a change in the amount of the maintenance order. In contrast, where no order for maintenance is given and there is no liberty to apply, the former wife no longer has the option of applying for maintenance in the future.

Previously, the court may award a nominal maintenance sum of one dollar to the former wife even if she earns more than her husband or is financially independent. This was to preserve the wife's right to maintenance and to give her a legal avenue to have the maintenance sum increased in the event of an adverse change in her circumstances.

In a shift from the traditional view, High Court Judge Choo Han Teck, in his decision, questioned if the basis for an unqualified right to maintenance by a woman in a divorce still stands in our society today. He expressed the need for a change in mindset in according financial protection to women

---

[63]*Supra* n 10, at s 114(1).

[64]*Supra* n 10, at s 114(1).

[65]*Minton v Minton* [1979] AC 593, quoted in *Lee Puey Hwa v Tay Cheow Seng* [1991] 3 MLJ 1.

where such protection is not required in instances where the former wife was in fact financially independent. He thus dismissed the woman's claim to maintenance without awarding a nominal sum to her as he found her to be financially independent throughout the marriage, having earned slightly more than her husband and accumulated significant assets of her own.[66]

This shift in perspective has been recently affirmed by the Singapore Court of Appeal which stated unequivocally that the courts cannot and ought not to order nominal maintenance automatically or as a matter of course to the former wife. A woman cannot simply argue that her situation might change in the future as it was not the duty of the courts to compensate parties for the vicissitudes of life nor the duty of the husband to act as a general insurer of his former wife for an indefinite period of time.[67] In this case, the court rescinded the award for nominal maintenance since it was clear from the facts and circumstances that the wife was more than capable of taking care of herself.

The duty to maintain a former wife or an incapacitated former husband ends upon his or her remarriage.[68] Hence, it can be said that the court takes the legal duty of former spouses seriously but in all cases, uses its judicial discretion, to ensure a fair outcome for both parties.

Maintenance of Former Husband

Previously, there was no corresponding duty to maintain the husband in the event of a divorce. With the latest amendments to the Women's Charter, the wife only has a corresponding duty to maintain the husband in the event of a divorce if he, during the marriage, is or becomes incapacitated due to any physical or mental disability, illness or from earning a livelihood and is and continues to be unable to maintain himself.[69] This continues to be a point for reform in the area of matrimonial law, particularly endorsed by Professor Leong Wai Kum, a leading family law academic. She argues that the law

---

[66]*ADB v ADC* [2014] SGHC 76.

[67]*ATE v ATD* [2016] SGCA 2.

[68]*Supra* n 10, at s 117.

[69]Amendment of Section 113 of the Women's Charter enacted by the Women's Charter (Amendment) Act 2016 which comes into effect in October 2016.

ought to be more in sync with the idea of marriage as an equal co-operative partnership of different efforts, and in line with this notion, that the duty of maintenance between spouses should be equal.[70]

Further, a legal duty to maintain the husband is arguably a stance more reflective of society today, particularly where women are progressively financially independent and contributions of a financial nature no longer stem solely from the husband. The idea of "house husbands" or stay-at-home fathers is no longer a foreign concept in modern day societies. It is left to be seen if Parliament will adopt such a stance in the years to come and further extend the scope of provision of maintenance to former husbands.

Maintenance of Child

A child is his or her parents' responsibility regardless of their marital status, especially because the law accepts that there is an inherent bond between each parent and their child. Hence, the termination of a marriage has no effect on the parents' equal and joint legal duty to provide for the child. This includes the provision of child maintenance.

An application made for a child maintenance order can be brought separately or together with the divorce proceedings. However, the latter option of a combined action might be preferred out of convenience.

Again, the court strives to safeguard the interests of the child and will take his or her welfare as the paramount consideration in determining a reasonable maintenance order. As with other maintenance orders discussed, some factors considered include the income, earning capacity and financial resources of the parents, the financial needs of the child, and all other obligations and responsibilities of the parties to the marriage, including responsibilities from a subsequent marriage.[71] However, one extra factor of interest is that the court will consider the manner in which the child is being educated at the time of the application, and how he or she will be brought up in the future.[72] This goes hand in hand with the outlook that a parent's

---

[70]Leong Wai Kum, "The Singapore Women's Charter: 50 Questions" (2011).

[71]*THG v LGH* [1996] 1 SLR(R) 767; [1996] SGHC 65.

[72]*Supra* n 10, at s 69(4)(g).

legal duty is to provide for his or her child having regard to the child's station in life.[73]

In the same vein, the current consensus of the court seems to find lump sum payment orders inappropriate in child maintenance cases even though it is an available legal option to pursue. The court is usually cautious when awarding a lump sum to avoid either over-compensating the child or providing a wholly inadequate award of maintenance especially as it is difficult to predict the child's needs in the future. If a monthly maintenance is awarded, it is open to either party to request for an increase or decrease in monthly maintenance depending on the circumstances at the time of the respective petitions. In this way, a periodic maintenance order appears to be a more reasonable and fair approach in safeguarding the welfare of the child.

Predicting the Unpredictable:[74]

A wife and her rich husband were getting a divorce. At the time of the proceedings, he was no longer working but was receiving a monthly pension and parent allowance from his daughter from his first marriage. His ex-wife requested for a lump sum maintenance payment for their seven-year-old child.

The court agreed with the husband that it was impossible to envisage what the young child's financial needs were likely to be for the next 14 years or even beyond. Awarding a lump sum payment would not allow the court to consider inter alia, the financial status of the parties in the years to come, the state of the child's health and his spending habits.

Following from the stance that parental responsibility rests on both parents, it has been argued that the duty to maintain the child ought to be imposed as much on the wife as on the husband.[75] This argument is particularly strong where the mother is working and self sufficient, that she

---

[73]*Id*, at s 68.
[74]Principles in *MB v MC* [2005] SGDC 181; Affirmed on appeal in *MB v MC* [2008] SGHC 246.
[75]*Supra* n 65.

should bear a legal obligation to contribute to the maintenance of her child rather than purely relying on her husband.[76]

Trials that concern child maintenance may be bitter, with most allegations stemming from mutual anger and distrust of the other party. The court is wary of taking allegations of misconduct at face value and where the situation allows for it, the court chooses to recognise that beneath the belligerence lies the hearts of two parents who genuinely love their child. Such a stance aligns with the court's inclination to make joint custody orders to ensure that the child has the opportunity to develop loving relationships with both parents.

The divorce process itself is an unpleasant topic to discuss in a marriage book but it is always better to be aware, spot the signs and find alternative ways of resolution before it is too late.

---

[76]*AFZ v AGB* [2008] SGDC 371.

Conclusion

Love is patient, love is kind. It does not envy, it does not boast, it is not proud. It does not dishonor others, it is not self-seeking, it is not easily angered, it keeps no record of wrongs. Love does not delight in evil but rejoices with the truth. It always protects, always trusts, always hopes, always perseveres. Love never fails.

— St. Paul

It is always easy to view relationships through rose-tinted glasses. Yet, the reality is that a marriage does not survive on romantic notions alone. It calls for hard sacrifices. Marriage can be quite a complicated affair, with many legal and financial consequences. From dealing with wealthy parents that demand that their future daughter or son-in-law sign a prenuptial agreement to protect their child's inherited assets, to a woman wishing to keep her maiden name, to family planning, to purchasing property, to discord within the family unit, there are many considerations for you and your partner both together and individually.

Ultimately, a marriage between two people is almost akin to an agreement between two parties. Like any legal agreement, there are certain legal rules and terms that must be followed or that are applied. It would not be wise to dismiss the law as irrelevant in a marriage. As made clear time and again throughout the span of this book, the law helps to set the perimeters of acceptable behaviour from the start of a relationship up to the marriage and beyond. Unlike a legal agreement, resolving the issues arising from a marriage does not merely concern the head but must be directed by the heart.

111

We hope that this book has provided you with a fresh insight into the impact the law can have on you and your partner. For the cynic, we hope that your reading of this book has allayed fears or at least spawned better understanding of what marriage entails. For the romantic, we hope to have imparted the idea that marriage has consequences and alerted him or her to these potential implications of a "spur of the moment" decision.

Family law is important because it affects everybody. It concerns the rights and obligations of husbands, wives, fathers, mothers, sons, daughters, uncles, aunts, nephews, nieces, grandfathers, grandmothers and so on. Each is affected in a different way. More significantly, Family Law is a malleable area of law that allows for outcomes that follow specifically from the circumstances of a particular situation. Accordingly, this book cannot, and is not meant to be, comprehensive. If you have a legal question or any concern on any topic, it is advisable to obtain legal advice from a lawyer, and/or visit a qualified counsellor.

ANNEX

WHAT I REALLY WANT TO KNOW ABOUT YOU*

- ☐ Do you want children? When? How many? How will they be disciplined?
- ☐ Have you previously been married or widowed or cohabited?
- ☐ Are you addicted to anything?
- ☐ Are there genetic diseases in your family or a history of cancer, heart disease, or chronic illness? Or any mental diseases?
- ☐ Do you follow a specific diet? Do you expect me to do the same?
- ☐ How important is it to you to contribute time or money to charity?
- ☐ Would you ever consider getting a vasectomy or having your tubes tied?
- ☐ Have you ever gambled? Smoked? Drunk? Done drugs? Pornography?
- ☐ How do you want to spend weekends and holidays together as a family unit?

- ☐ How do you feel about divorce?
- ☐ Is there anything about your past that I don't know, but should be aware of?
- ☐ Where will we live? Will we live with your parents?
- ☐ How do you see our lives in twenty years?
- ☐ Do you have children from any previous marriage(s) or non-marital relationship(s)? Are you supporting them financially?
- ☐ What are your religious views? Do you share my religious views?
- ☐ Who will be responsible for paying the bills on time?
- ☐ Have you ever had a serious illness? Have you ever had surgery?
- ☐ Have you ever committed a crime, been arrested, or been in jail?
- ☐ What is your love language? Physical touch; acts of service; words of affirmation; quality time or giving gifts?

- ☐ Is there some activity you are not prepared to give up in a marriage?
- ☐ Would you expect me to work full-time?
- ☐ How many hours a week do you work? Have you ever been called a workaholic?
- ☐ How often will we have sex?
- ☐ If we have troubles in our relationship, are you willing to go for marital counselling or mediation?
- ☐ Would you be willing to support a sick child?
- ☐ Are you a virgin? If not, have you always practised safe sex?
- ☐ How will household chores be divided? Are we getting a maid?
- ☐ If you or I were offered a job opportunity in another country, would you move?
- ☐ Do you have a sexually transmitted disease? Have you been tested?

- ☐ What percentage of your income is spent/saved every month?
- ☐ What is your view of abortion?
- ☐ If you could, what is one thing you would change about me?
- ☐ How much time will we spend with the in-laws? How much maintenance will we contribute to our parents?
- ☐ Do you want a family pet?
- ☐ Do you want to have a joint account or separate accounts or both? Will we hold all assets jointly?
- ☐ Do you consider yourself liberal, moderate, conservative, or non-political?
- ☐ What are your expectations of marriage?

---

*A checklist of points that couples could discuss with each other and be comfortable about before they commit to marriage.

About Yeo-Leong & Peh LLC

Yeo-Leong & Peh LLC was first established in 1987 and has developed since its humble beginnings into one of the larger law corporations in Singapore today.

Through our experiences with a wide range of clients, we have cultivated an international perspective and the ability to meet needs of clients not only in Singapore but also in Asia, Europe and USA. Our clients benefit from our own in-house Chinese legal advisor who is equipped to provide research and support on the Chinese legal system and industry practice. Yeo-Leong & Peh's ability to assist clients in cross-border legal services is also complemented by its membership of LAWorld — a network of over 50 independent law firms across 47 countries worldwide.

We are able to provide services in the following principal areas of law:

Banking and Corporate Transactions
Banking Litigation and Debt Recovery
Company Incorporation, Corporate Secretarial and Maintenance Services
Conveyancing and Real Estate
Cross Border Legal Services
Family Law including Marriage & Divorce, Adoption, Succession, Probate, Wills and Trust
General Litigation, Arbitration Mediation and Dispute Resolution
Immigration and Employment Law
Information Technology
Intellectual Property
Mergers & Acquisitions, Listings

Shipping and Admiralty
Public and Private International Law

Yeo-Leong & Peh LLC's ethos is to discharge our work with integrity and courage at the highest standard achievable. Beyond our legal practice, we also wish to grow as a member of the community and to make a lasting contribution to the lives of our clients.

About the Author

Jennifer Yeo is the founder and senior partner of YEO-LEONG & Partners, a law firm which she set up in 1987 as a sole proprietorship which later became Yeo-Leong & Peh, a partnership. She became the chairman when the firm became a limited liability law corporation known as YEO-LEONG & PEH LLC on 1 April 2002. It now has about 170 employees and a licensed representative office in Shanghai. In the course of her work, she has advised and represented public and private companies, banks and individuals from all walks of life in their acquisition, financing and disposal of commercial and residential buildings, lands and development projects, public listing, asset securitisation, various aspects of banking business and operations (including lending activities), joint ventures and acquisitions and corporate agreements, probates, wills and family law matters. She serves as an independent director in a company listed on the Main Board of the Singapore Stock Exchange.

Jennifer graduated with LLB (Hons) from National University of Singapore in 1981 and with LLM in Banking Law Studies from Boston University in 1985. She was given the Outstanding Student Award in 1985 and the Outstanding Alumni Award in 2013 by Boston University. She is an Advocate & Solicitor of the Supreme Court of Singapore and was called to the Singapore Bar in 1982. She is also a Solicitor of England and Wales and was admitted in 1999. She is a fellow of the Singapore Institute of Arbitrators and the Chartered Institute of Arbitrators. She also used to practise as a mediator with the Singapore Mediation Center.

She is the founder and Chairman of VIVA Foundation for Children with Cancer, an institution of public character and charity established in Singapore in 2005 to raise the cure rate of children with cancer in Singapore and the region. She is also founder & Chairman of VIVA China Children's Cancer Foundation Ltd set up in 2014, a charity in HK committed to raise the cure rate of childhood cancer in China & Hong Kong. She served as a member of the Board of Governors, Raffles Girls' Secondary School for more than 10 years, chaired the South Asia chapter of the Urban Land Institute, and served as the director of the Assisi Hospice for a few years.

She is literate in English and Malay and can speak some Mandarin and Chinese dialects.

She enjoys travelling and music. She is Licentiate of the Royal Schools of Music in Piano Performing (1975) and in Teaching (1978). She won the Phillips Award (First Prize Open Section) of the Singapore Musical Society's Annual Piano Competition in 1977. Her composition 'Keindahan Taman' entered the finals of the National Song Writing Competition 1977 and has been performed and recorded by a prominent artiste and choir on television and on CD. Jennifer has played Chopin's Piano Concertos No. 1 (Romance) and No. 2 (Larghetto) with the Singapore Symphony Orchestra under the batons of Maestros Bart Folse and Shui Lan respectively at benefit concerts to raise funds for the Singapore Symphony Orchestra Endowment Fund.

She is married to George Yeo the former Minister of Foreign Affairs of Singapore and currently Chairman of Kerry Logistics Network listed on the Hong Kong Stock Exchange. They have a daughter and three sons aged 27, 26, 25 and 23. They are a Roman Catholic family.